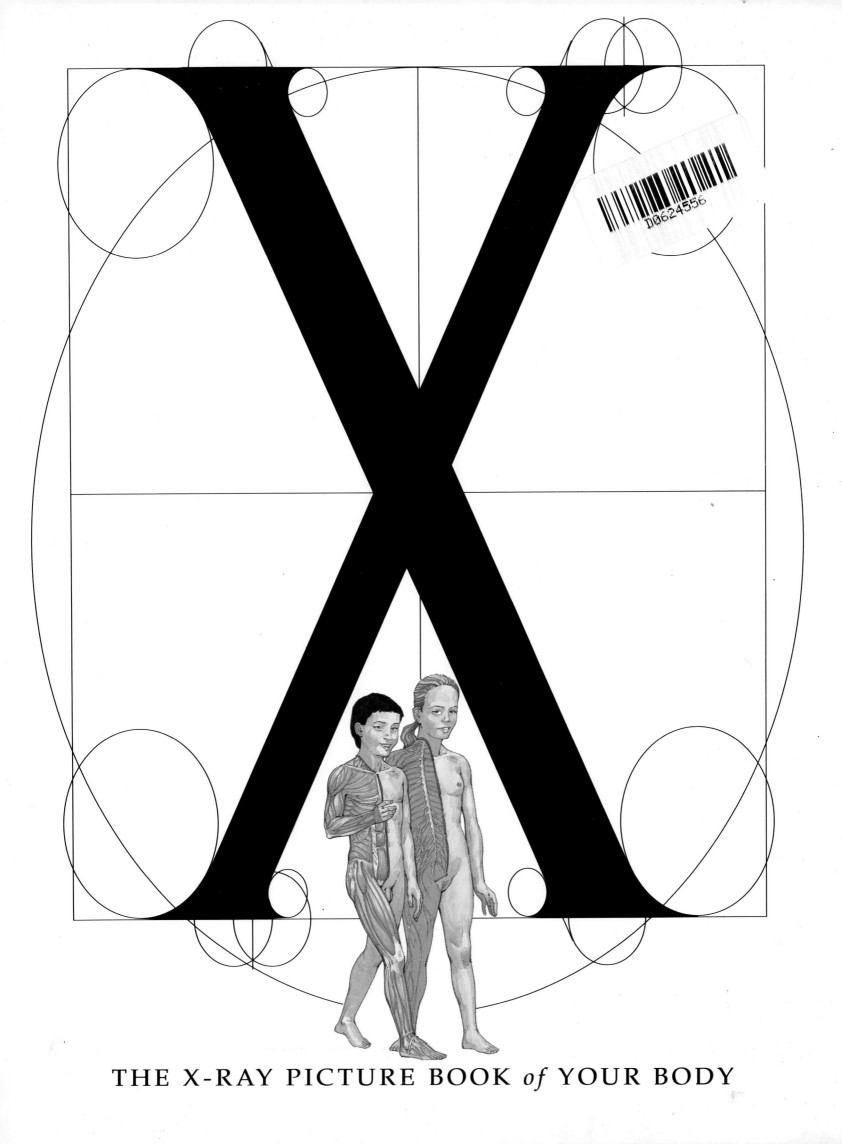

THE X-RAY PICTURE BOOK *of* YOUR BODY

Author:

Dr. Kathryn Senior is a former biomedical research scientist who studied at Cambridge University for a degree in pathology and a doctorate in microbiology. After four years in research she joined the world of publishing, working as an editor of children's science books. She has written **Medicine** in the *Timelines* series. Dr. Senior is now a freelance writer and editor living in Berkshire.

Creator:

David Salariya was born in Dundee, Scotland, where he studied illustration and printmaking, concentrating on book design in his postgraduate year. He has illustrated a wide range of books on botanical, historical, and mythical subjects. He has designed and created the *Timelines*, *New View*, and *X-ray Picture Book* series for Franklin Watts. He lives in Brighton with his wife, the illustrator Shirley Willis.

Consultant:

Dr. Philip Sawney trained as a cellular biologist and immunologist before studying medicine. He has worked in hospitals and in general practice. In addition, he has been a senior clinical medical officer in Community Health, specializing in services for the disabled. He was recently the consultant on a series of books on health-related subjects for teenagers and has written articles on a wide range of medical matters. Dr. Sawney lives in Kingston upon Thames.

Franklin Watts
95 Madison Avenue
New York, NY 10016

Library of Congress Cataloging-in-Publication Data
Senior, Kathryn.
    Your Body / written by Kathryn Senior;
created and designed by David Salariya.
      p. cm. – (The X-ray picture book)
    Includes index.
    ISBN 0-531-14336-8
    1. Human anatomy – Atlases – Juvenile literature.
    I. Salariya, David. II. Title. III. Series.
    QM27.S46 1994
    612–dc20
                                        93-40314
                                        CIP AC
Printed in Belgium

All rights reserved

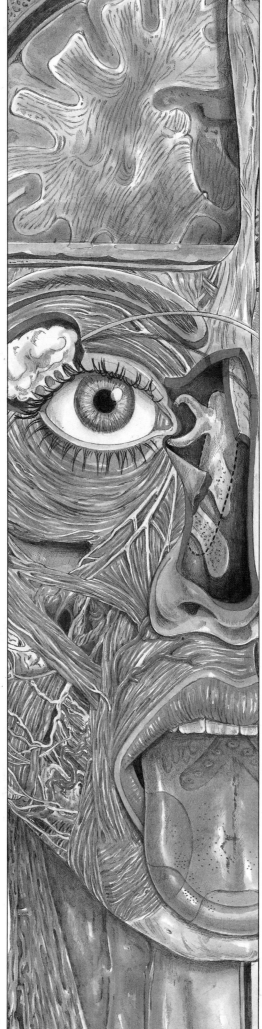

David Salariya   *Series Editor*
Ruth Taylor   *Senior Editor*
Diana Holubowicz   *Book Editor*
Dr. Philip Sawney   *Consultant*

Artists:

Mark Bergin
Ronald Coleman
John James
Sarah Kensington
Carolyn Scrace

Artists

Mark Bergin 28-29, 34-35; **Ronald Coleman** 18-19; **John James** 6-7, 12-13, 22-23, 32-33, 40-41; **Sarah Kensington** 30-31, 42-43; **Carolyn Scrace** 8-9, 10-11, 14-15, 16-17, 20-21, 24-25, 26-27, 36-37, 38-39, 44-45.

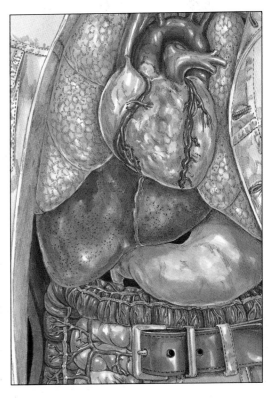

© The Salariya Book Co Ltd 1993

The X-RAY
PICTURE BOOK of
YOUR BODY

Written by
KATHRYN SENIOR

Created and designed by
DAVID SALARIYA

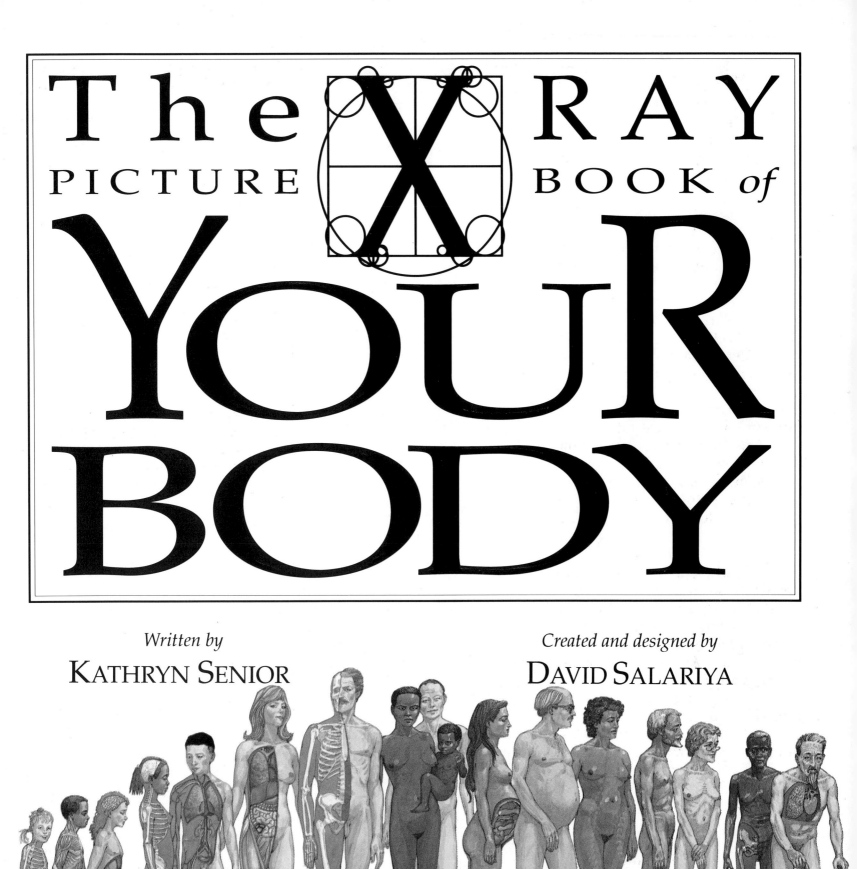

FRANKLIN WATTS

NEW YORK · CHICAGO · LONDON · TORONTO · SYDNEY

CONTENTS

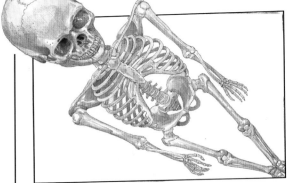

INTRODUCING THE BODY

SEX AND REPRODUCTION

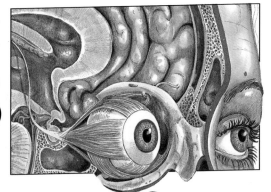

THE DIGESTIVE SYSTEM

THE NERVOUS SYSTEM

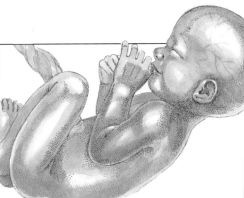

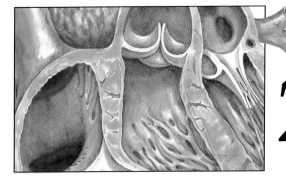

THE CIRCULATORY SYSTEM

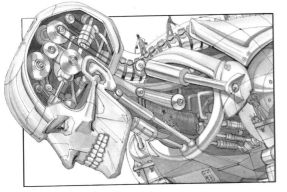

THE IMMUNE SYSTEM

THE IMMUNE SYSTEM is your body's defense mechanism. It mounts surveillance operations to spot invaders such as viruses and bacteria and battles to protect the body.

LOOKING AT THE BODY

YOUR BODY thrives under the pressure of exercise and sports. It also needs to rest – the average body needs about 8 hours sleep per night and becomes ill if deprived of sleep.

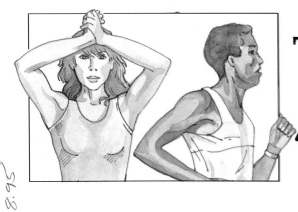

CARING FOR THE BODY

YOUR BODY needs plenty of exercise, good food, rest, and regular cleaning to stay healthy. Your body feels better and works better if you do not smoke or drink alcohol.

WHEN THE BODY FAILS

THE BODY'S DEFENSE and repair mechanisms can be overwhelmed. Sometimes medical technology can help, and many people now live to 80 and beyond.

THE CUSTOMIZED BODY

YOUR BODY is always changing. It evolved to its present form over thousands of years. Within its lifetime, each person's body can be changed by exercise and decoration.

INTRODUCING THE BODY
BODY SYSTEMS

The skeleton is a complex piece of engineering which gives the body strength and flexibility.

The digestive system spans several organs. Digestion of food begins as it is chewed in the mouth.

The nervous system is made up of the brain and spinal cord, 43 major nerves and many smaller ones.

The brain is the starting point of 12 major nerve pairs; the other 31 pairs start in the spinal cord.

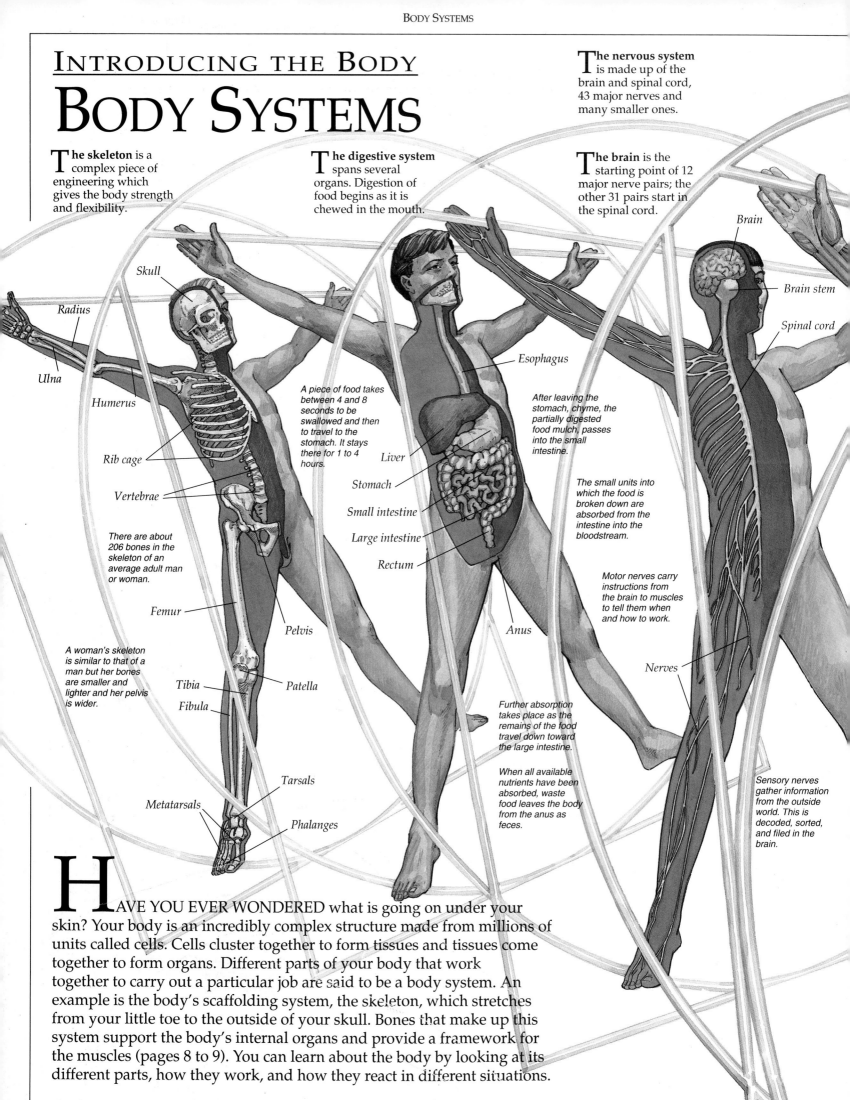

Skull

Radius

Ulna

Humerus

Rib cage

Vertebrae

A piece of food takes between 4 and 8 seconds to be swallowed and then to travel to the stomach. It stays there for 1 to 4 hours.

There are about 206 bones in the skeleton of an average adult man or woman.

Femur

A woman's skeleton is similar to that of a man but her bones are smaller and lighter and her pelvis is wider.

Pelvis

Tibia

Patella

Fibula

Tarsals

Metatarsals

Phalanges

Esophagus

Liver

Stomach

Small intestine

Large intestine

Rectum

After leaving the stomach, chyme, the partially digested food mulch, passes into the small intestine.

The small units into which the food is broken down are absorbed from the intestine into the bloodstream.

Anus

Further absorption takes place as the remains of the food travel down toward the large intestine.

When all available nutrients have been absorbed, waste food leaves the body from the anus as feces.

Brain

Brain stem

Spinal cord

Motor nerves carry instructions from the brain to muscles to tell them when and how to work.

Nerves

Sensory nerves gather information from the outside world. This is decoded, sorted, and filed in the brain.

HAVE YOU EVER WONDERED what is going on under your skin? Your body is an incredibly complex structure made from millions of units called cells. Cells cluster together to form tissues and tissues come together to form organs. Different parts of your body that work together to carry out a particular job are said to be a body system. An example is the body's scaffolding system, the skeleton, which stretches from your little toe to the outside of your skull. Bones that make up this system support the body's internal organs and provide a framework for the muscles (pages 8 to 9). You can learn about the body by looking at its different parts, how they work, and how they react in different situations.

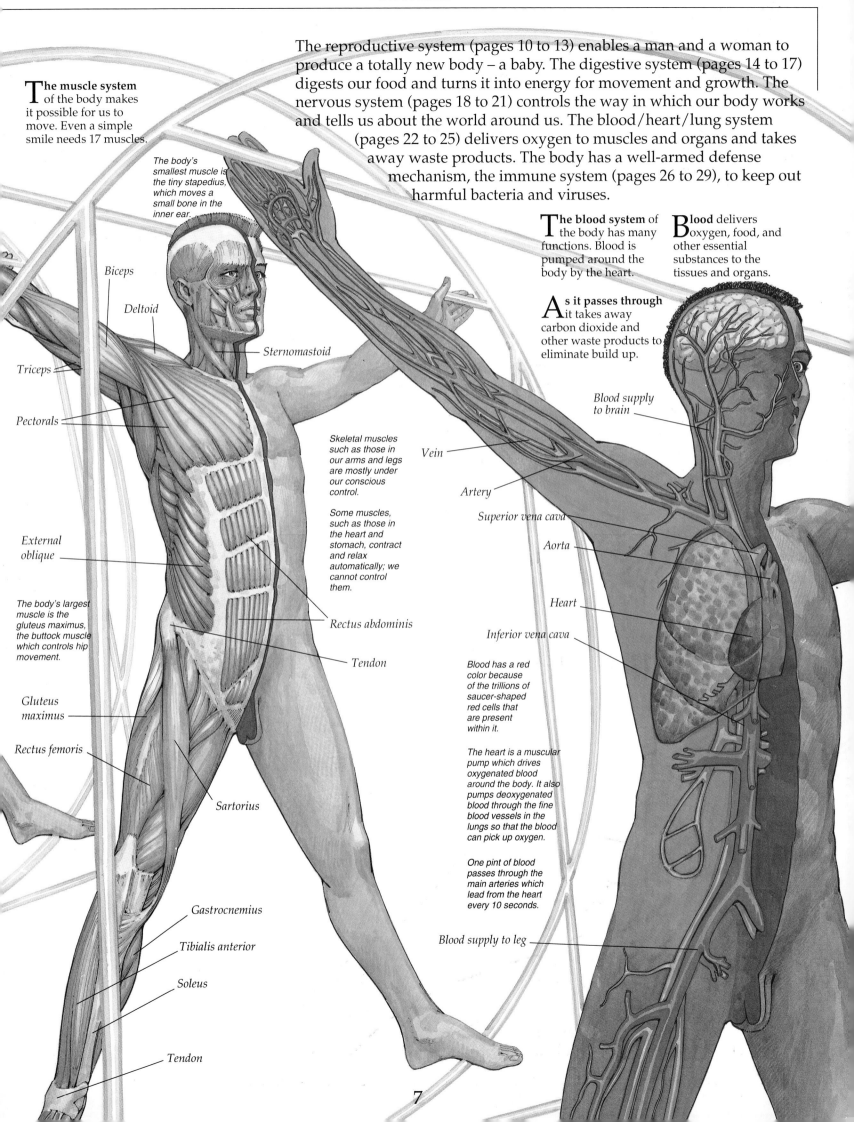

The reproductive system (pages 10 to 13) enables a man and a woman to produce a totally new body – a baby. The digestive system (pages 14 to 17) digests our food and turns it into energy for movement and growth. The nervous system (pages 18 to 21) controls the way in which our body works and tells us about the world around us. The blood/heart/lung system (pages 22 to 25) delivers oxygen to muscles and organs and takes away waste products. The body has a well-armed defense mechanism, the immune system (pages 26 to 29), to keep out harmful bacteria and viruses.

The muscle system of the body makes it possible for us to move. Even a simple smile needs 17 muscles.

The body's smallest muscle is the tiny stapedius, which moves a small bone in the inner ear.

Biceps

Deltoid

Triceps

Pectorals

Sternomastoid

External oblique

Skeletal muscles such as those in our arms and legs are mostly under our conscious control.

Some muscles, such as those in the heart and stomach, contract and relax automatically; we cannot control them.

The body's largest muscle is the gluteus maximus, the buttock muscle which controls hip movement.

Rectus abdominis

Gluteus maximus

Tendon

Rectus femoris

Sartorius

Gastrocnemius

Tibialis anterior

Soleus

Tendon

The blood system of the body has many functions. Blood is pumped around the body by the heart.

Blood delivers oxygen, food, and other essential substances to the tissues and organs.

As it passes through it takes away carbon dioxide and other waste products to eliminate build up.

Blood supply to brain

Vein

Artery

Superior vena cava

Aorta

Heart

Inferior vena cava

Blood has a red color because of the trillions of saucer-shaped red cells that are present within it.

The heart is a muscular pump which drives oxygenated blood around the body. It also pumps deoxygenated blood through the fine blood vessels in the lungs so that the blood can pick up oxygen.

One pint of blood passes through the main arteries which lead from the heart every 10 seconds.

Blood supply to leg

INTRODUCING THE BODY
THE BODY'S SKELETON

Your body is held together by a skeleton made from bone, tendons, and ligaments. The skeleton acts as scaffolding to support muscles and organs. Bone has the strength of wrought iron and the flexibility of soft wood. Bones are not solid but have a honeycomb structure. This gives them strength but also lightness. Bones are jointed in several places in the body, at the elbow and knee, for example. Joints work with muscles to allow the body to move.

Tendons connect muscles to bones. A tendon as thick as a pencil can bear a weight of 1,000 lbs (453 kg).

Tendons in the hand are protected from wear and tear by fluid-filled sacs called tendon sheaths.

Tendon sheaths

Tendon

Radius

Extensor retinaculum

Muscles

Tendon sheaths

Carpal

Metacarpal

Distal phalanx

Middle phalanx

Proximal phalanx

Hinged synovial joint

The hand is made up of 26 bones. Each finger has three bones and three hinged synovial joints.

Tendons

Teeth

Lower jaw

Clavicle

Scapula

Sternum

Shoulder joint

Synovial fluid

Vertebrae

Humerus

Humerus

Muscle

Sacrum

Coccyx

Carpals

Metacarpals

Phalange

Tibia

Fibula

Tarsal

Metatarsal

Phalange

There are two main types of joint in the body. Synovial, or mobile, joints like the shoulder allow a large range of movement. Fibrous, or fixed, joints such as the joints between bones in the skull permit little or no movement.

Sesamoid bones are so called because they look like large sesame seeds.

The adult skeleton contains 206 separate bones. A new-born baby has more than this – about 270. Many of these fuse as the child grows.

The fingernail itself is a dead structure formed from the same material as hair. A fingernail grows at a rate of 1 inch (2.6 cm) per year – 4 times faster than a toenail.

Nail body

Lunula

Cuticle

Nailbed

Nail root

Finger bone

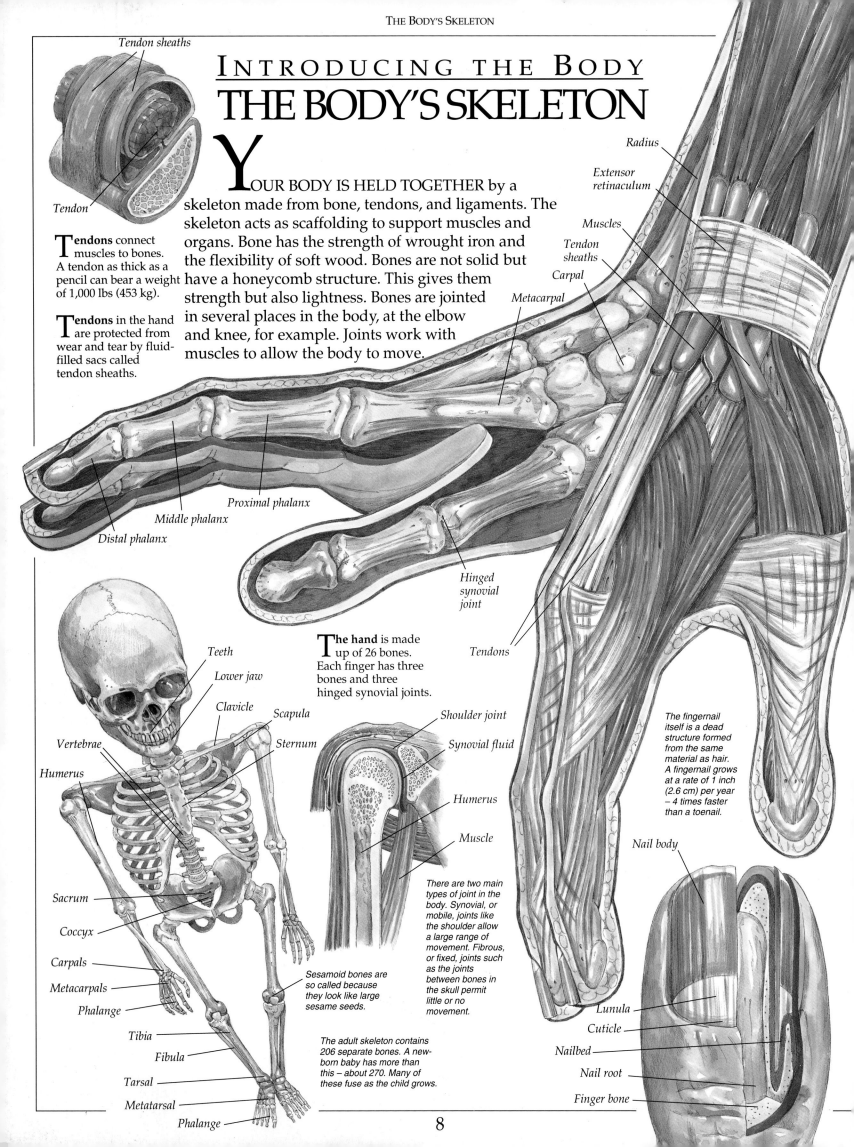

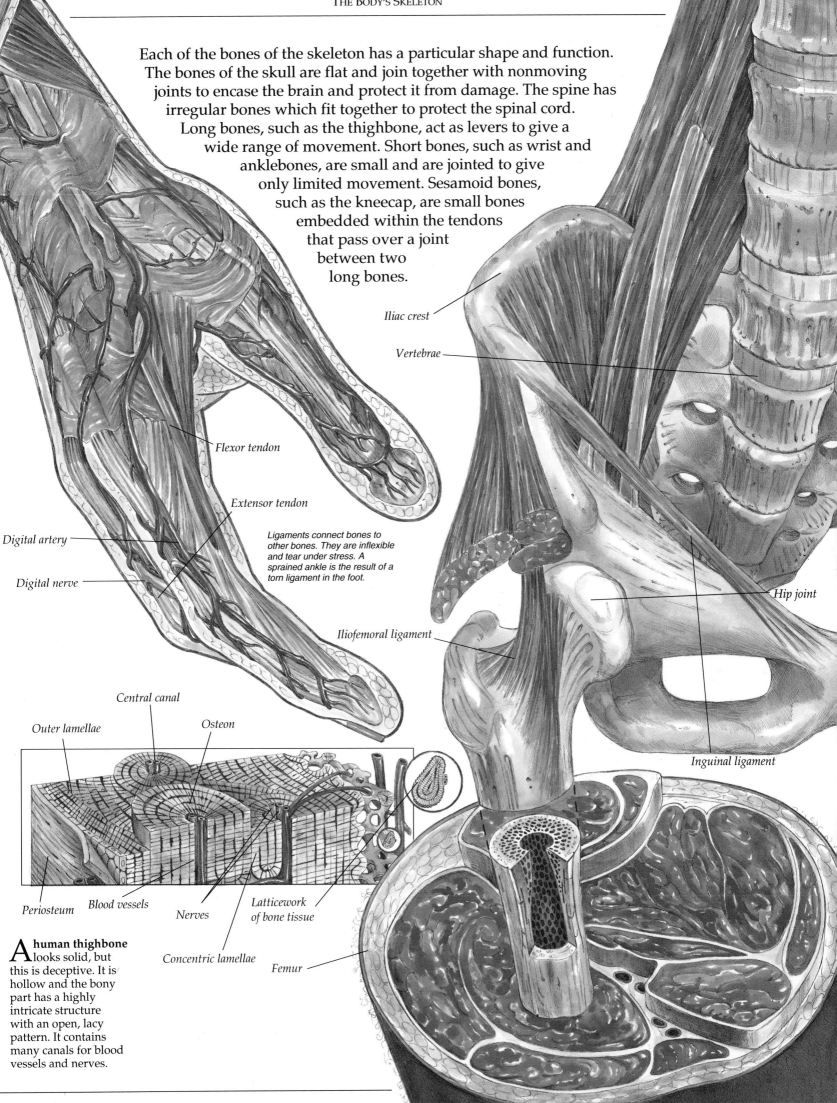

Each of the bones of the skeleton has a particular shape and function. The bones of the skull are flat and join together with nonmoving joints to encase the brain and protect it from damage. The spine has irregular bones which fit together to protect the spinal cord. Long bones, such as the thighbone, act as levers to give a wide range of movement. Short bones, such as wrist and anklebones, are small and are jointed to give only limited movement. Sesamoid bones, such as the kneecap, are small bones embedded within the tendons that pass over a joint between two long bones.

Iliac crest

Vertebrae

Flexor tendon

Extensor tendon

Ligaments connect bones to other bones. They are inflexible and tear under stress. A sprained ankle is the result of a torn ligament in the foot.

Digital artery

Digital nerve

Hip joint

Iliofemoral ligament

Inguinal ligament

Central canal

Outer lamellae

Osteon

Periosteum   *Blood vessels*

Nerves

Latticework of bone tissue

Concentric lamellae

Femur

A human thighbone looks solid, but this is deceptive. It is hollow and the bony part has a highly intricate structure with an open, lacy pattern. It contains many canals for blood vessels and nerves.

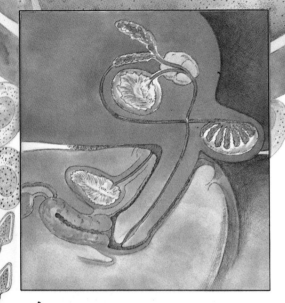

Nucleus

Fertilization happens when the head of a sperm gets inside the egg and fuses with its nucleus.

— *Mitochondria*

— *Head of sperm*

— *Midsection of sperm*

— *Tail of sperm*

BEFORE BIRTH

THE TIME FROM CONCEPTION TO BIRTH is about 266 days. Pregnancy starts when an egg is fertilized by a sperm. The resulting cell divides and embeds itself in the wall of the mother's uterus. In the first three months of pregnancy the mother-to-be does not change shape, but the baby inside her develops rapidly. By the time the mother first notices the bump in her abdomen, at about week fourteen of pregnancy, her baby is fully formed but is too tiny to live outside her uterus.

From being a ball of cells it has become a recognizable human being with a face, arms and legs, and fingers and toes. Its heart is beating, its brain and nervous system are present, and its muscles and sexual organs are continuing to grow. The baby moves around constantly but the mother cannot yet feel it.

When a man and a woman have sex, the man's sperm is released into the woman's vagina.

About 400 million sperm begin the journey into the uterus but only one fertilizes the egg.

Polar body

Zona pellicuda

Nucleus

Blastomere

Nucleus

1st division: 2 cells

2nd division: 4 cells

Morula

A day and a half after fertilization the fused egg and sperm, the zygote, divides to make two cells.

The cells carry on dividing and by day 5 a ball of cells, the morula, has formed.

Umbilical cord

Head

Leg bud

Eye

Spinal cord

Arm bud

Spine

Rib

Blood vessels

Eye

Ear

Heart

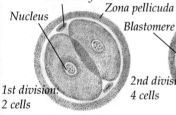

Fertilized egg

Uterus

Egg

Ovary

A mature egg is pushed out of an ovary in about 72 seconds. When egg and sperm meet, fertilization takes 300 seconds.

At 4 weeks after fertilization the baby is about 7 mm long. Its heart beats and its spine and nervous system are beginning to form. It does not yet look like a human baby.

By week 16 the baby is about 5 in (14 cm) long. Its limbs grow and fingernails and toenails begin to develop. It is covered by fine hair called lanugo. This usually disappears before birth.

Fallopian tube

During the first week after conception, the fertilized egg travels down the Fallopian tube and, by day 7, implants into the wall of the uterus.

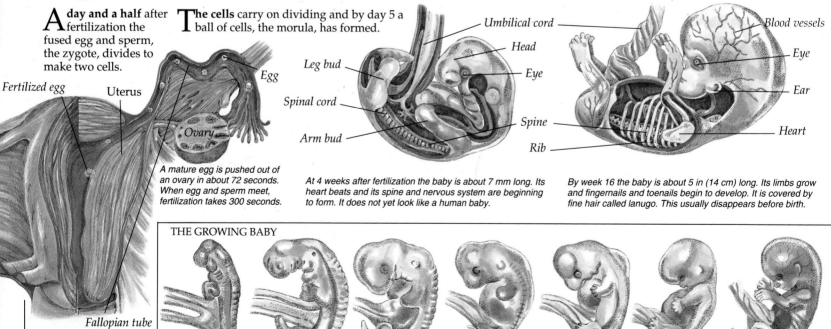

THE GROWING BABY

24 days old length is 3 mm

28 days old length is ¼ in (7 mm)

5 weeks old length is ½ in (1 cm)

6 weeks old length is ¾ in (1.3 cm)

7 weeks old length is 1 in (2 cm)

8 weeks old length is 1½ in (4 cm)

12 weeks old length is 4 in (10 cm)

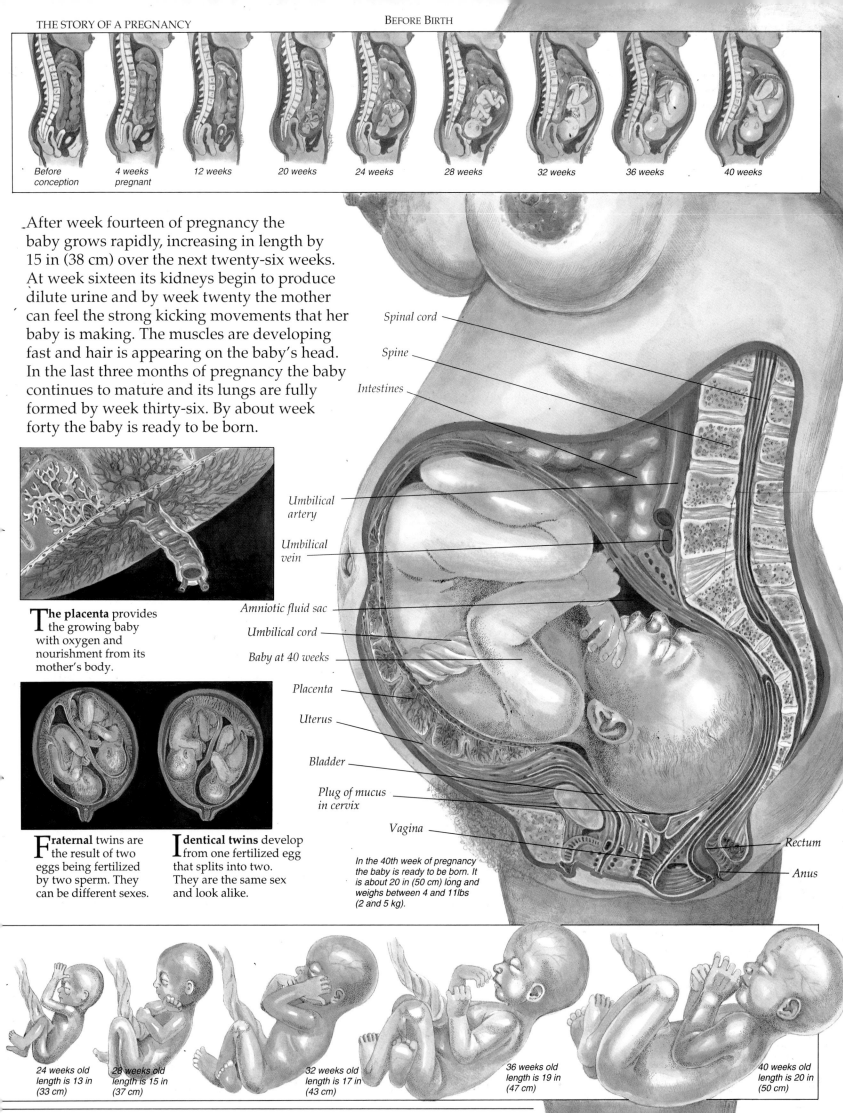

| Before conception | 4 weeks pregnant | 12 weeks | 20 weeks | 24 weeks | 28 weeks | 32 weeks | 36 weeks | 40 weeks |

After week fourteen of pregnancy the baby grows rapidly, increasing in length by 15 in (38 cm) over the next twenty-six weeks. At week sixteen its kidneys begin to produce dilute urine and by week twenty the mother can feel the strong kicking movements that her baby is making. The muscles are developing fast and hair is appearing on the baby's head. In the last three months of pregnancy the baby continues to mature and its lungs are fully formed by week thirty-six. By about week forty the baby is ready to be born.

The placenta provides the growing baby with oxygen and nourishment from its mother's body.

Fraternal twins are the result of two eggs being fertilized by two sperm. They can be different sexes.

Identical twins develop from one fertilized egg that splits into two. They are the same sex and look alike.

Spinal cord
Spine
Intestines
Umbilical artery
Umbilical vein
Amniotic fluid sac
Umbilical cord
Baby at 40 weeks
Placenta
Uterus
Bladder
Plug of mucus in cervix
Vagina
Rectum
Anus

In the 40th week of pregnancy the baby is ready to be born. It is about 20 in (50 cm) long and weighs between 4 and 11lbs (2 and 5 kg).

24 weeks old length is 13 in (33 cm)

28 weeks old length is 15 in (37 cm)

32 weeks old length is 17 in (43 cm)

36 weeks old length is 19 in (47 cm)

40 weeks old length is 20 in (50 cm)

THE STORY OF A BIRTH

1

2

3

4

5

1 After 9 months of pregnancy the baby is ready to be born.

2 The uterus makes strong squeezing movements.

3 The mother's cervix opens and the baby moves down.

4 The head is usually born first, followed by the body.

A few minutes later, the uterus contracts again.

5 The placenta is pushed out of the mother's body.

SEX AND REPRODUCTION
GROWING UP

Hypothalamus

Milk glands

Nipple

Milk ducts

A HUMAN BABY is dependent on its parents for food and warmth at birth. It instinctively searches for its mother's breast and sucks. Breastmilk contains all the food that the baby needs in the first few months of its life. At about six months old, the first teeth begin to show through the gums and the baby starts to eat food which has been mashed up into a puree. As the months pass, the baby grows and matures. Its body weight triples in the first year after birth and its height doubles. The nervous system continues to develop and the child begins to sit up and, later, to walk and talk. Bones and muscles grow and the child matures and enters adolescence.

When a baby sucks at its mother's breast, signals are sent to her brain. Part of it, the hypothalamus, then releases chemicals which tell the breast to produce fluid. A yellow liquid called colostrum is produced in the first 3 days after birth. This protects the baby from infection because it is rich in antibodies from the mother's blood. Mature milk, which looks watery and bluish in color, is produced within 3 to 10 days of birth.

1

2

3

4

5

6

1 Between the ages of 6–10 months babies can sit up, and generally take a lot of interest in the things going on around them.

2 At six months to 1 year old they begin crawling movements and by 12 to 14 months can take a few faltering steps.

3 Within 6 months, at the age of about 18 months, they are moving around much more confidently and can say a few simple words.

4 At the age of 3 the body and limbs are lengthening and the brain and nervous system are maturing rapidly. Coordination is now good.

5 When a child starts school at the age of 4 or 5 he or she has a full set of 20 milk teeth. These are later replaced by adult teeth.

6 At the age of 7 the brain begins to produce sex hormones and these rise in concentration over the next 5 years.

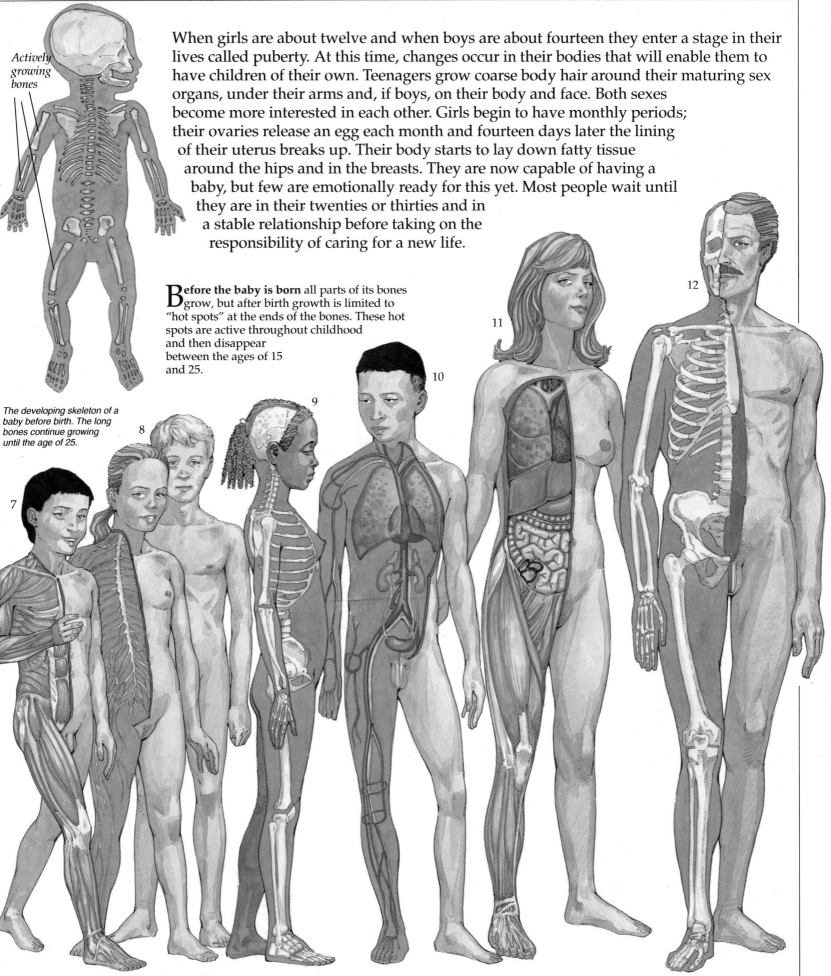

When girls are about twelve and when boys are about fourteen they enter a stage in their lives called puberty. At this time, changes occur in their bodies that will enable them to have children of their own. Teenagers grow coarse body hair around their maturing sex organs, under their arms and, if boys, on their body and face. Both sexes become more interested in each other. Girls begin to have monthly periods; their ovaries release an egg each month and fourteen days later the lining of their uterus breaks up. Their body starts to lay down fatty tissue around the hips and in the breasts. They are now capable of having a baby, but few are emotionally ready for this yet. Most people wait until they are in their twenties or thirties and in a stable relationship before taking on the responsibility of caring for a new life.

Actively growing bones

Before the baby is born all parts of its bones grow, but after birth growth is limited to "hot spots" at the ends of the bones. These hot spots are active throughout childhood and then disappear between the ages of 15 and 25.

The developing skeleton of a baby before birth. The long bones continue growing until the age of 25.

7

8

9

10

11

12

7
The rate of growth of the bones slows down between the ages of 7 and 10 and then speeds up again just before puberty.

8
Children start puberty at different ages. If their diet is poor and they are underweight puberty may be delayed.

9
At puberty the sex organs in both sexes mature and secondary changes occur; a girl develops breasts and a boy's voice changes.

10
After puberty the body matures into full adulthood. The long bones stop growing and muscular strength is built up.

11
Between the ages of 18 and 25 a man is at his sexual and muscular peak. A woman's fertility is at its greatest when she is 28.

12
Some parts of the adult body – hair, skin, nails – all grow actively throughout life. The lining of the stomach replaces itself every 3 days.

EATING AND DRINKING

ALL YOUR FOOD AND DRINK is taken into your body through the mouth. When you eat a sandwich, the piece that you have bitten into becomes moistened by saliva. Your tongue pushes the food into the teeth for chewing and molds the softened and fragmented piece of sandwich into a ball. The mucus in your saliva coats the ball, lubricating it and making it easier to swallow. The digestive process has already begun; enzymes in the saliva have started to break down carbohydrates in the bread, such as starch, and are converting them to glucose. This needs to happen so that the food can be absorbed into the body – glucose molecules are small and easily absorbed, but a large carbohydrate, like starch, cannot pass from the intestines into the blood.

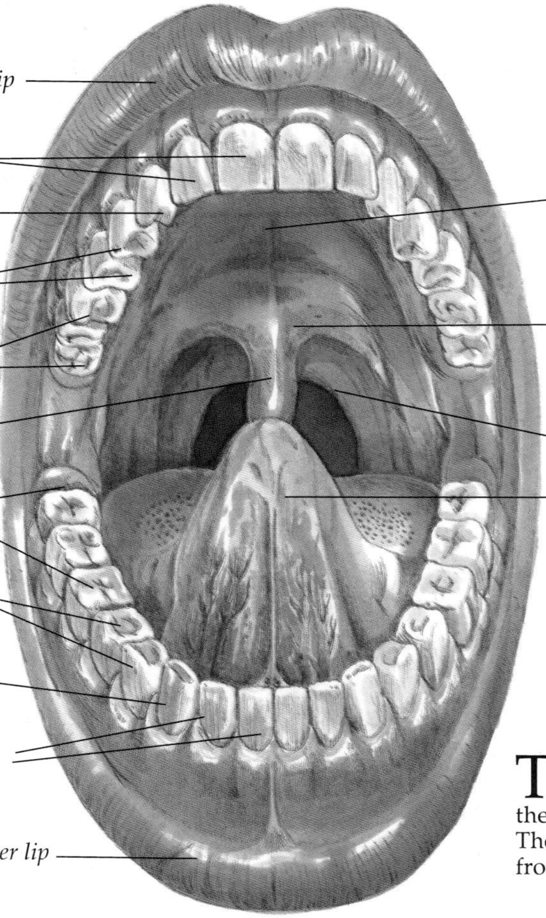

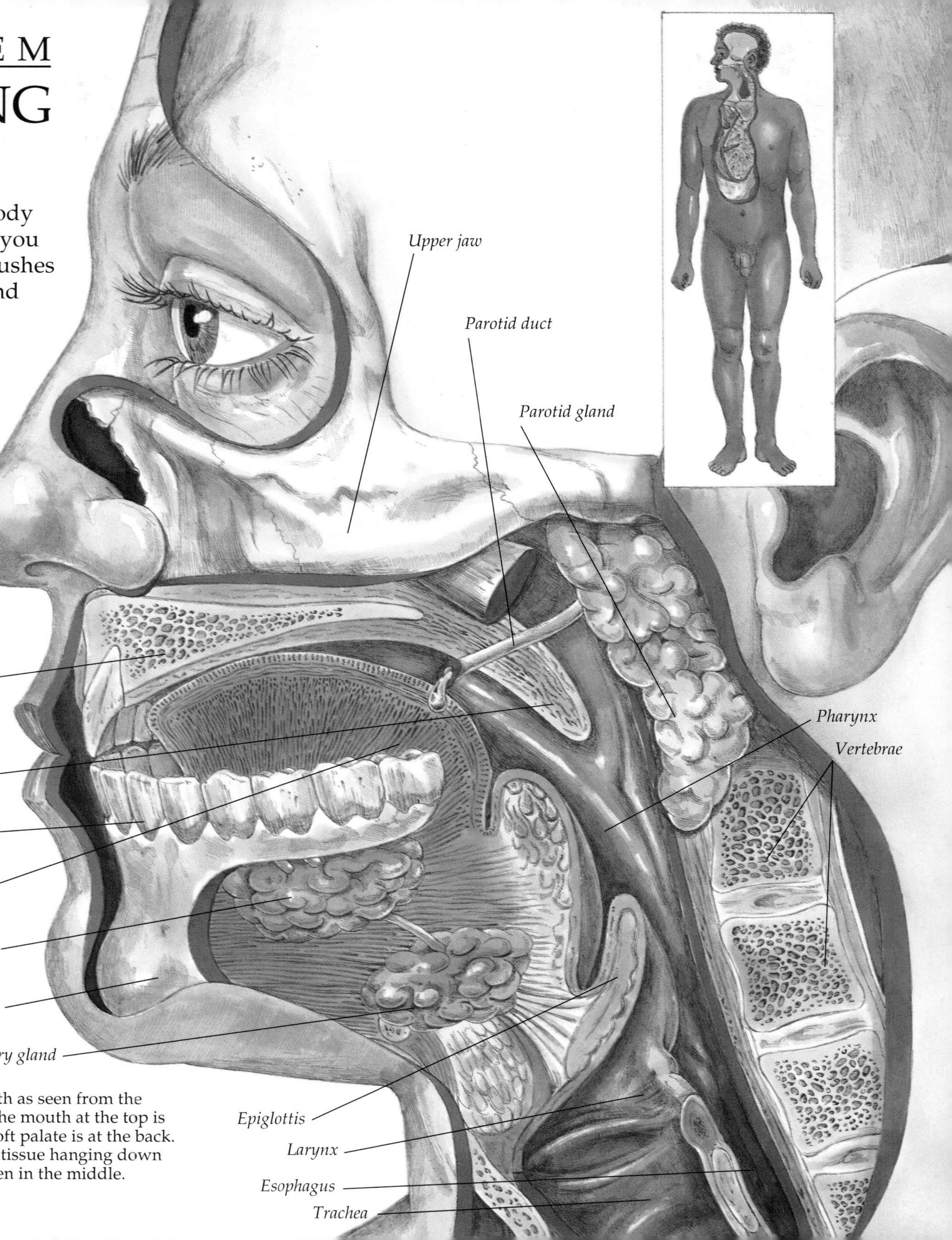

The view inside a mouth as seen from the front. At the front of the mouth at the top is the hard palate and the soft palate is at the back. The uvula, a soft piece of tissue hanging down from the soft palate, is seen in the middle.

Pharynx

Vertebrae

Parotid gland

Parotid duct

Upper jaw

Epiglottis

Larynx

Esophagus

Trachea

Hard palate

Soft palate

Teeth

Tonsils

Tongue

Salivary gland

Lower jaw

Salivary gland

Upper lip

Incisors

Canine

Premolars

Molars

Uvula

Molars

Premolars

Canine

Incisors

Lower lip

14

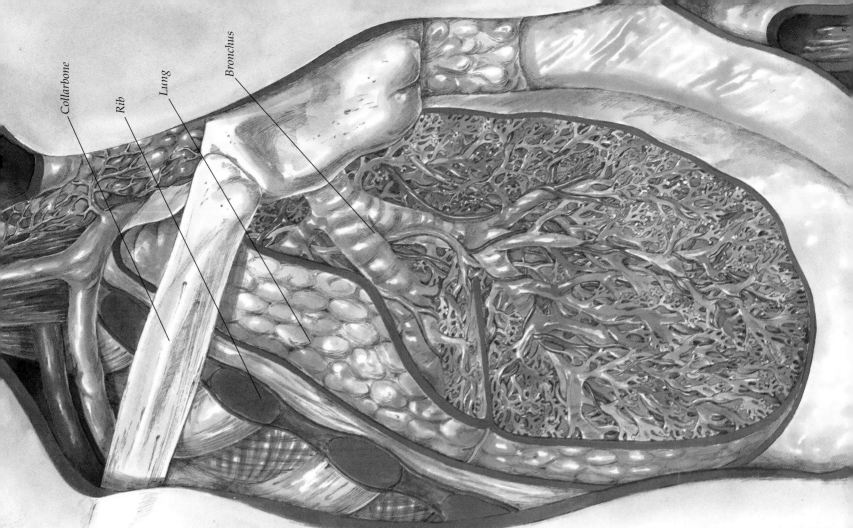

Collarbone

Rib

Lung

Bronchus

Teeth first appear in the fetus six weeks after conception. The milk teeth have come through by the age of 3 and various adult teeth emerge from the gums at the age of 6 (first molars), 12 (second molars) and 18 (the wisdom teeth).

Teeth play an important role in digesting food. Most adults have 32 permanent teeth.

There are 4 incisors, 2 canines, 4 premolars, and 6 molars in the upper and in the lower jaw.

Each type of tooth has a different function: incisors slice food, canines tear into it, and molars grind it.

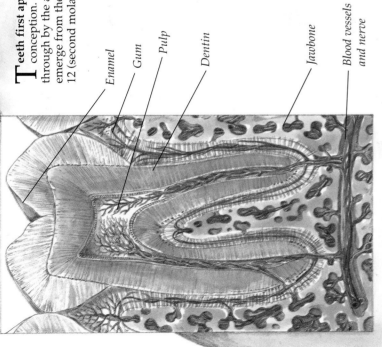

Enamel

Gum

Pulp

Dentin

Jawbone

Blood vessels and nerve

The process of chewing and swallowing also gives you the opportunity to enjoy the flavors in different types of food and drink. Thousands of taste buds, specialized patches of cells on the tongue and soft palate, send signals to the brain when certain types of food are chewed.

Different regions of the mouth detect different flavors. Sweet and salty flavors are picked up at the front of the tongue; sour and bitter flavors are detected at the back of the tongue and also on the palate. The taste buds that detect bitterness are by far the most sensitive. They can sense this flavor at a concentration of 1 part in 2 million. The cells that detect a sweet flavor can only do so when it is 400,000 times more concentrated.

The first phase of digestion ends when the tongue pushes the ball of chewed and moistened food into the back of the throat. This part of swallowing is under our conscious control. The food is then swallowed automatically; squeezing actions of the throat muscles push the food into the pharynx.

The muscles of the pharynx contract and push the food toward the esophagus. The tongue keeps the food from going back into the mouth and the soft palate and epiglottis keep the food from going into the nose or the windpipe. The muscles of the esophagus squeeze the food into the stomach in an action called peristalsis.

THE DIGESTIVE SYSTEM
THE FANTASTIC FOOD JOURNEY

W HEN THE SANDWICH you swallowed on pages 14 to 15 reaches the bottom of the esophagus, it falls into an acid-filled reservoir, the stomach. The juice that is produced by the stomach lining also contains enzymes to continue digesting the food. When the sandwich has been thoroughly pulped, it is forced out of the other end of the stomach and into the small intestine. More digestive enzymes produced in the gall bladder and pancreas are released into the intestine. These break down the sandwich into very small units which are absorbed into the bloodstream. The blood takes them to other parts of the body to be used as fuel for muscles and organs. The mixture of water, undigestible material, and bacteria then leaves the small intestine and enters the large intestine.

The tube that forms the digestive system is, in total, about 28 feet (8.5 m) long in an average adult.

Food moves along the intestine because the musles in the walls contract and relax continuously.

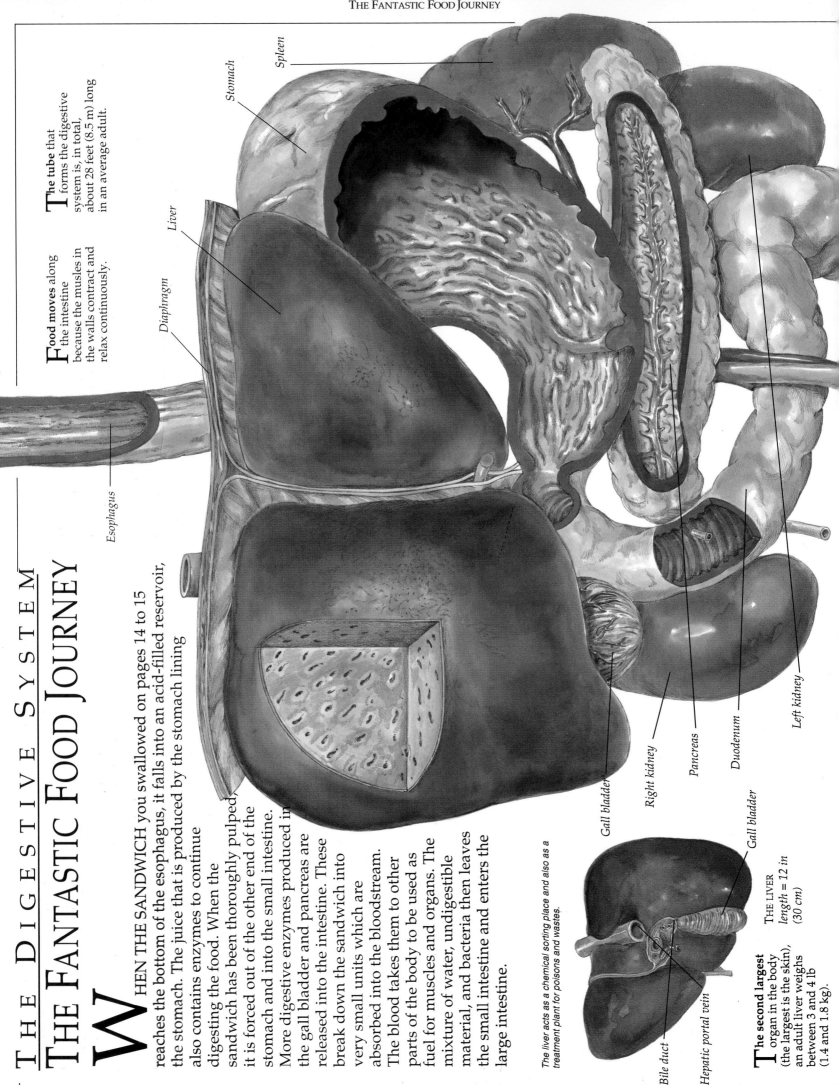

Spleen

Stomach

Liver

Diaphragm

Esophagus

Gall bladder

Right kidney

Pancreas

Duodenum

Left kidney

Gall bladder

Bile duct

Hepatic portal vein

The liver acts as a chemical sorting place and also as a treatment plant for poisons and wastes.

THE LIVER
length = 12 in
(30 cm)

The second largest organ in the body (the largest is the skin), an adult liver weighs between 3 and 4 lb (1.4 and 1.8 kg).

The colon is the longest section of the large intestine; it measures over 4 feet (about 1.3 m) in an average adult. The other sections are called the cecum, the rectum, and the anus.

Rectum

Anal sphincter

Anus

Blood vessels

The appendix is a small sac which seems to have no real function. It can become inflamed.

If this happens, appendicitis results and a simple operation must be performed to remove the appendix.

Appendix

Cecum

Colon

Coiled jejunum and ileum

Ureter

Renal capsule

Medulla

Renal vein

Renal artery

Renal pelvis

Cortex

Pyramid

Layers of stomach muscle

Stomach lining

Pyloric sphincter

THE STOMACH
length = 8 in
(20 cm)

THE KIDNEY
length = 3 in (8 cm)

The stomach is a flexible bag made from muscle. When we are hungry it contracts strongly, each contraction lasting 2 or 3 minutes. The squeezing of air and gastric juice produces the well-known noise of your stomach rumbling.

When proteins are broken down during the digestive process waste products containing nitrogen are formed. These are poisonous to the body and must be gotten rid of, or excreted. This is a function of the liver and kidneys.

As the last of the sandwich goes through your large intestine, it becomes feces. Feces lose water as they pass along the colon, becoming solid waste. When expelled from the body feces are 75% water and 25% solid material. A third of this is dead bacteria (some bacteria live in the colon to help digest food), a third is undigested fats and proteins, and one third is fiber (the part of plant food which contains cellulose and which cannot be digested). The feces pass from the colon into the rectum. They are released from the anus when the anal sphincter is opened. Although you cannot control the movement of the feces in the colon, the opening of this ring of muscle is usually under your conscious control.

THE NERVOUS SYSTEM
THINKING AND FEELING

Your BODY PICKS UP INFORMATION about the world via receptors in your skin and via sense organs in your head. This information is transmitted along nerves to other parts of the body and to the body's central computer, the brain. Nerves are complex bundles of specially designed cells. The twelve pairs of major nerves which arise in the brain and the thirty-one pairs that arise in the spinal cord contain both sensory and motor fibers. Each major nerve branches many times to form an elaborate network of peripheral nerves which spread throughout the body.

Sensory nerves transmit messages from the body to the spinal cord and brain. Motor nerves send messages back to tell muscles and other tissues what to do.

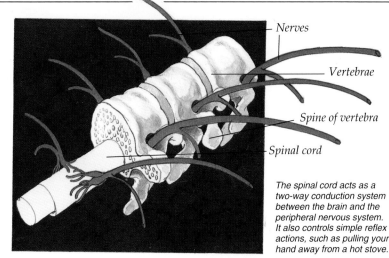

Nerves
Vertebrae
Spine of vertebra
Spinal cord

The spinal cord acts as a two-way conduction system between the brain and the peripheral nervous system. It also controls simple reflex actions, such as pulling your hand away from a hot stove.

Lung
Bronchus
Esophagus
Liver
Stomach

Mesenteric ganglia

Colon

Adrenal gland

Appendix

Kidney

Ureter

Rectum

Anus

Bladder

Lumbar vertebrae

Sacral vertebrae

Autonomic messages from your brain and spinal cord are relayed to the body by nerve masses called ganglia. The main diagram, above right, shows the pattern of nerves which form the autonomic nervous system and represents the ganglia as satellites. The ganglia work in a similar way to communication satellites, in that they receive messages from an information source, the brain, and then relay them to information receivers, the organs. The whole of the autonomic nervous system is controlled by the hypothalamus (pages 20 to 21). This receives information about variations in the body's systems and acts to bring them back into balance.

Coccyx

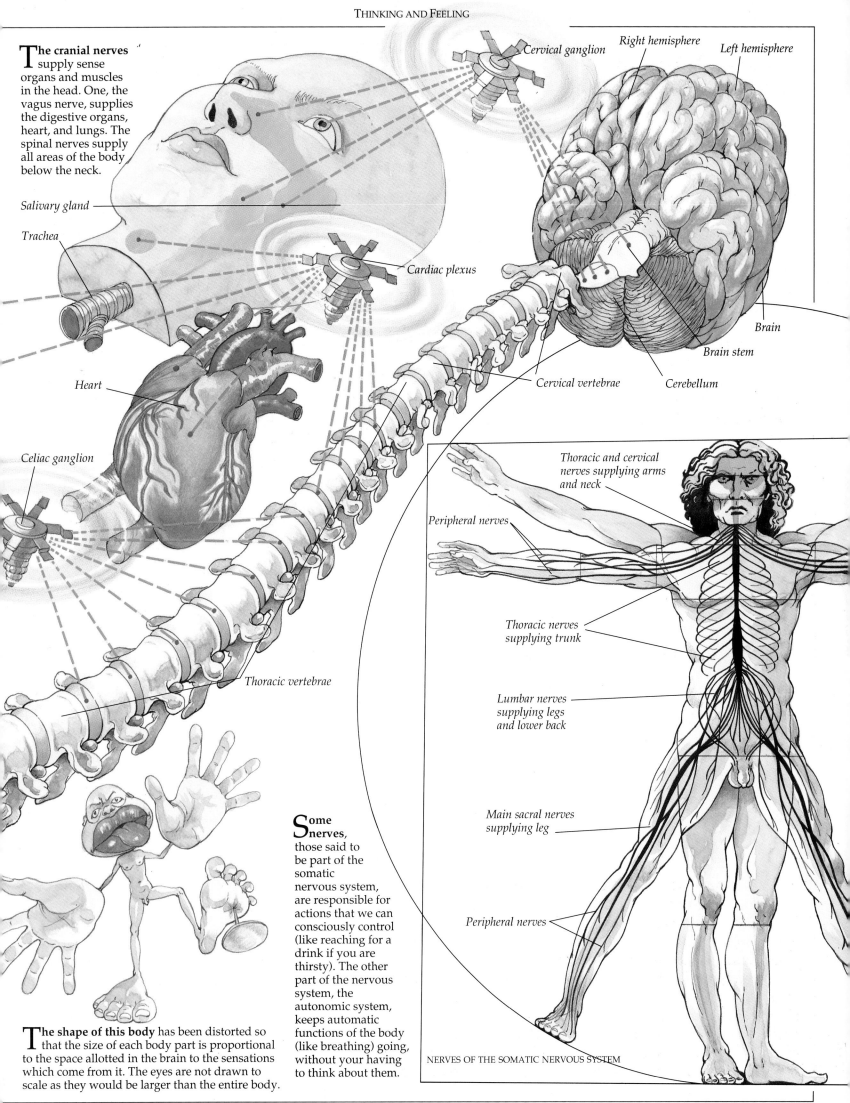

The cranial nerves supply sense organs and muscles in the head. One, the vagus nerve, supplies the digestive organs, heart, and lungs. The spinal nerves supply all areas of the body below the neck.

Salivary gland

Trachea

Heart

Celiac ganglion

Thoracic vertebrae

Cervical ganglion

Cardiac plexus

Cervical vertebrae

Right hemisphere

Left hemisphere

Brain

Brain stem

Cerebellum

Thoracic and cervical nerves supplying arms and neck

Peripheral nerves

Thoracic nerves supplying trunk

Lumbar nerves supplying legs and lower back

Main sacral nerves supplying leg

Peripheral nerves

Some nerves, those said to be part of the somatic nervous system, are responsible for actions that we can consciously control (like reaching for a drink if you are thirsty). The other part of the nervous system, the autonomic system, keeps automatic functions of the body (like breathing) going, without your having to think about them.

The shape of this body has been distorted so that the size of each body part is proportional to the space allotted in the brain to the sensations which come from it. The eyes are not drawn to scale as they would be larger than the entire body.

NERVES OF THE SOMATIC NERVOUS SYSTEM

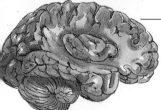

THE NERVOUS SYSTEM
THE BODY'S COMPUTER

THE BRAIN is your body's computer. It receives information from receptors in the skin and in some of the internal organs. The sense organs – the eye, the ear, the tongue, and the nose – also provide plenty of data. The brain decodes and sorts this information and then sends out messages along nerves in the spinal cord to tell organs and muscles what to do.

You are able to understand complicated ideas, to remember things, and to think. The cerebrum, the larger outer part of the brain, is involved in these more complex functions, but we do not know exactly how it works.

When you listen to a sound your eardrum and the bones inside your ear vibrate. The vibrations are transmitted through the cochlea to the auditory nerve. This sends the sound message to the brain for decoding.

The cerebrum is the largest, most complex structure in your brain. It is divided into two distinct halves called hemispheres. These are further divided into four lobes. The temporal lobes are associated with the senses of hearing and smell, the parietal lobes with touch and taste, the occipital lobes with sight, and the frontal lobes with movement, speech, and complex thought.

A BRAND NEW BRAIN

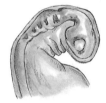
day 23 after conception

week 4

week 7

week 10

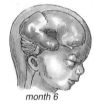
week 14

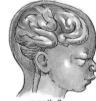
month 6

month 8

newborn baby

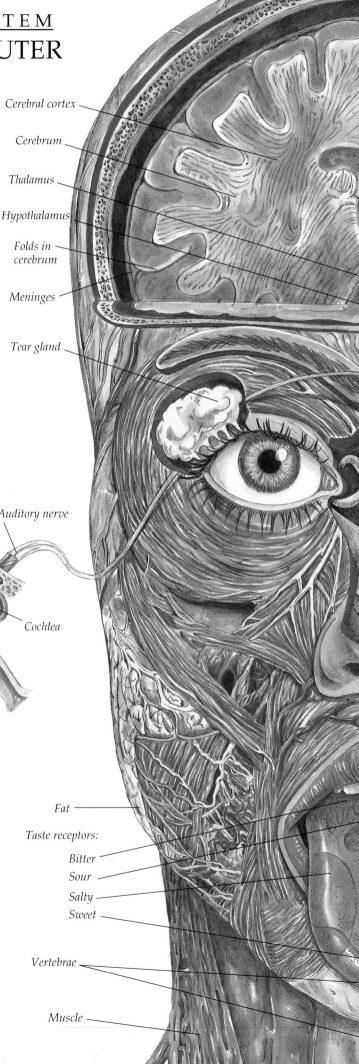

Cerebral cortex

Cerebrum

Thalamus

Hypothalamus

Folds in cerebrum

Meninges

Tear gland

Bony canal

Semicircular canals

Auditory nerve

Cochlea

Pinna

Eardrum

Ossicles

Fat

Taste receptors:

Bitter

Sour

Salty

Sweet

Vertebrae

Muscle

The thalamus and the hypothalamus are two important brain structures which lie at the base of your brain, under the two cerebral hemispheres. The thalamus acts like a telephone exchange between the spinal cord and the cerebrum. The hypothalamus is the part of the brain that controls vital functions such as eating, sleeping, and body temperature. It is linked directly to the pituitary gland and indirectly to the organs of the body which produce hormones such as growth and sex hormones.

Scalp

Skull

Forehead

Frontal lobe

Optic nerve

Muscles that move eyeball

Pupil

Iris

Eyeball

Hard palate

Soft palate

Lip

Hyoid bone

Mandible

Larynx

Chin

Trachea

Esophagus

C.S.GRACE.

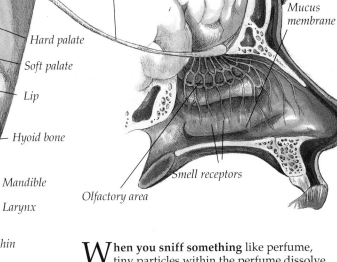

Eyeball

Optic nerves

Nerve fibers

Optical chiasma

The eye is the body's camera. Light that bounces off the objects around you passes into your eye through the pupil. It is focused onto the back of the eye where special cells convert the picture into nerve signals. These go to the brain for decoding.

Olfactory nerve

Mucus membrane

Smell receptors

Olfactory area

When you sniff something like perfume, tiny particles within the perfume dissolve into the mucus inside your nose. This excites special cells in the nasal cavity and these pass messages on to the brain via nerves.

THE CIRCULATORY SYSTEM
THE BLOOD

A healthy adult takes a week to produce enough new red blood cells to replace those in a pint of blood which has been donated.

An average man has 5 to 6 quarts/liters of blood.

An average woman has 4 to 5 quarts/liters of blood.

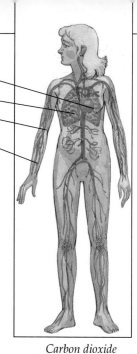

Heart
Lungs
Veins
Arteries

Though HE CIRCULATORY SYSTEM OF YOUR BODY is a transport system. It consists of a network of blood vessels through which blood travels to all parts of the body. The center of the system is the heart, a muscular pump (pages 24 to 25). Blood contains red blood cells and white blood cells. White blood cells help to protect the body from bacteria and viruses (pages 26 to 29). Red blood cells carry oxygen from the lungs to the tissues, and carbon dioxide from the tissues back to the lungs. The rest of the blood, the plasma, is mainly water and transports materials such as food, waste, and hormones.

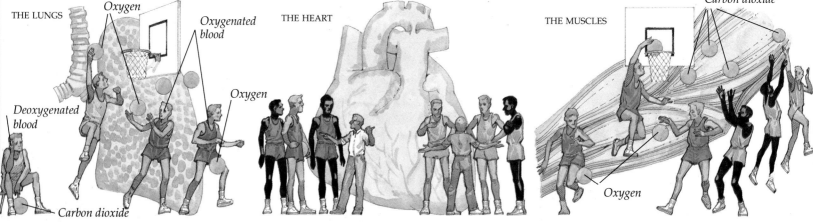

THE LUNGS

Oxygen

Oxygenated blood

Deoxygenated blood

Oxygen

Carbon dioxide

In blood vessels in the lungs, deoxygenated blood (represented by the blue basketball team) gives up carbon dioxide, so that it can be breathed out. The blood then picks up oxygen, becoming oxygenated blood (represented by the red basketball team).

THE HEART

Oxygenated blood (the red team) travels from the lungs to the heart. From there it is pumped to the body by the left ventricle (represented by the red coach). Deoxygenated blood also travels to the heart and is pumped to the lungs by the right ventricle (represented by the blue coach), to pick up oxygen.

THE MUSCLES

Carbon dioxide

Oxygen

In the muscles, oxygenated blood (the red team) gives up its oxygen to the muscle cells. This enables them to burn up food fuel in order to make the body move. As it leaves, the deoxygenated blood (the blue team) picks up carbon dioxide and other waste, which is discarded by the muscle cells.

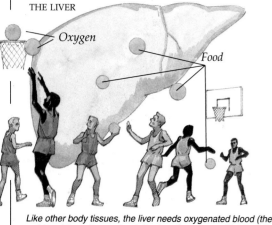

THE LIVER

Oxygen

Food

Like other body tissues, the liver needs oxygenated blood (the red team) to make regular deliveries of oxygen so that its cells can work efficiently. Deoxygenated blood (the blue team), which has picked up digested food from the intestine, passes this to the liver, before returning to the heart.

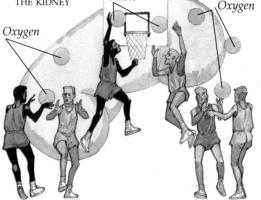

THE KIDNEY

Waste

Oxygen

Oxygen

Oxygenated blood (the red team) also delivers oxygen to the kidney so that its cells can burn up food energy. Deoxygenated blood (the blue team) drops off the chemical wastes (mainly urea) which it has picked up from other tissues. The kidney then excretes these wastes in the urine.

Blood travels around the body carrying many different materials. These drawings illustrate what your blood does in five different places in your body, using two basketball teams to represent your blood. The red team represents oxygenated blood and the blue team deoxygenated blood.

The temperature of blood in the body is about 98°F (38°C).

The life span of a red blood cell is about 120 days.

There are 6 types of mature white blood cell.

Each cubic millimeter of blood contains 4 to 6 million red blood cells.

Oxygen is needed by every cell in your body to enable it to burn up food fuel for energy. Oxygenated blood is sent out to the body from the heart. It delivers its oxygen when it reaches the organs and muscles and becomes deoxygenated. The red blood cells in deoxygenated blood pick up carbon dioxide and take it back to the lungs. Blood plasma, which flows near to the intestines, picks up digested food units (pages 14 to 17) and delivers them to the liver for processing. Waste, such as urea, is delivered to the kidneys. Hormones such as growth hormone are taken from their site of production in the pituitary gland to where they are needed.

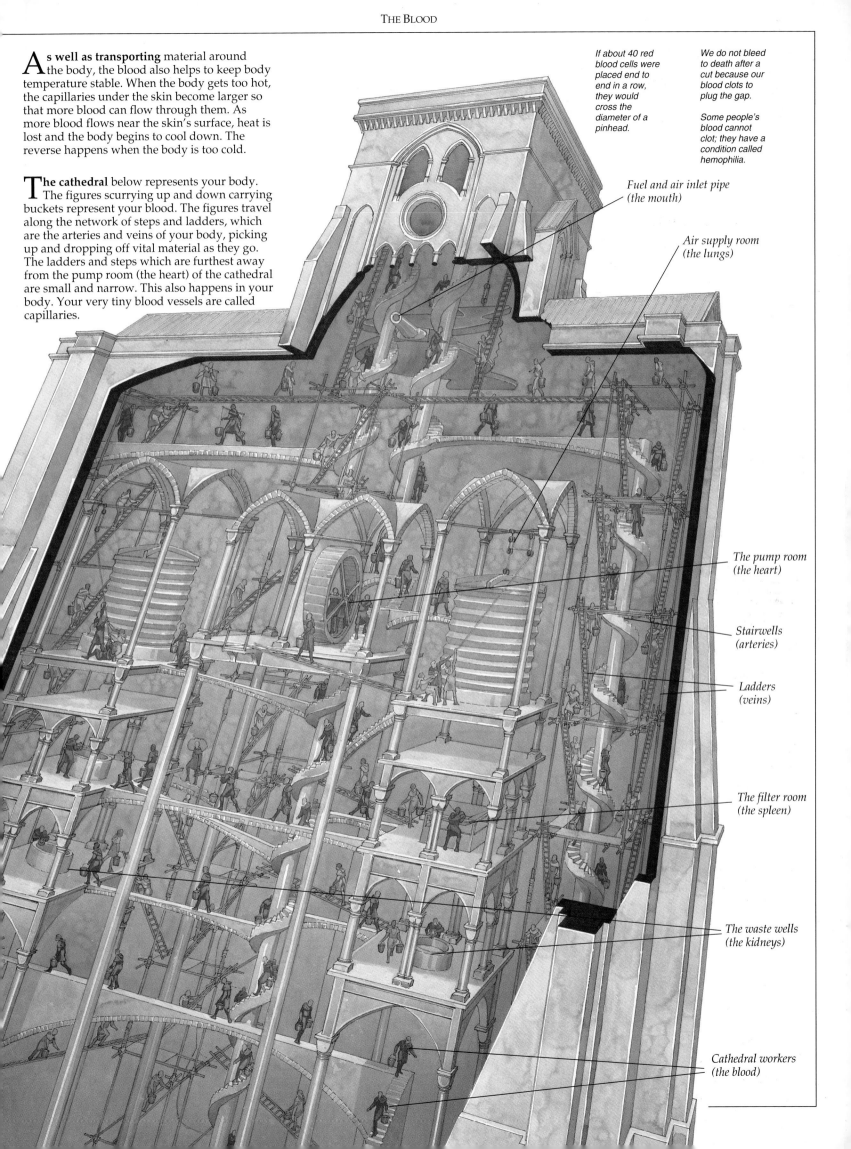

As well as transporting material around the body, the blood also helps to keep body temperature stable. When the body gets too hot, the capillaries under the skin become larger so that more blood can flow through them. As more blood flows near the skin's surface, heat is lost and the body begins to cool down. The reverse happens when the body is too cold.

The cathedral below represents your body. The figures scurrying up and down carrying buckets represent your blood. The figures travel along the network of steps and ladders, which are the arteries and veins of your body, picking up and dropping off vital material as they go. The ladders and steps which are furthest away from the pump room (the heart) of the cathedral are small and narrow. This also happens in your body. Your very tiny blood vessels are called capillaries.

If about 40 red blood cells were placed end to end in a row, they would cross the diameter of a pinhead.

We do not bleed to death after a cut because our blood clots to plug the gap.

Some people's blood cannot clot; they have a condition called hemophilia.

Fuel and air inlet pipe
(the mouth)

Air supply room
(the lungs)

The pump room
(the heart)

Stairwells
(arteries)

Ladders
(veins)

The filter room
(the spleen)

The waste wells
(the kidneys)

Cathedral workers
(the blood)

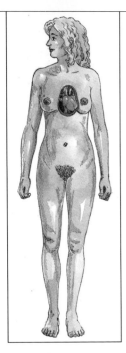

THE CIRCULATORY SYSTEM
THE HEART

YOUR HEART is a pump that has four chambers. Its job is to pump blood around the body so that the blood can transport vital materials to and from different organs.

Every body cell, whether in a muscle or an organ or a nerve, needs a constant supply of oxygen and other materials. It must also have carbon dioxide and other wastes taken away for disposal. Blood which has been to the tissues is low in oxygen and high in carbon dioxide and travels through the veins back to the heart. It goes through the right side of the heart and is pumped to the lungs to lose its carbon dioxide and to pick up oxygen. Oxygenated blood returns to the left side of the heart and is then pumped to the tissues from the left ventricle.

Superior vena cava

Aorta

Aortic valve

Tricuspid valve

Right atrium

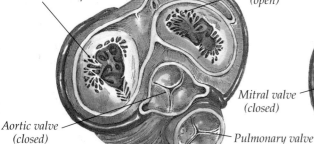

Mitral valve (open)

Tricuspid valve (open)

Mitral valve (closed)

Aortic valve (closed)

Pulmonary valve (closed)

Tricuspid valve (closed)

Aortic valve (open)

Pulmonary valve (open)

Valve leaflet

Across-section of the heart valves, viewed from the top. The tricuspid and mitral valves are open and blood flows into the ventricles. The aortic and pulmonary valves are closed and no blood flows into the pulmonary artery or the aorta.

Later in the heartbeat cycle, the mitral and tricuspid valves slam shut and the aortic and pulmonary valves open. Blood is forced into the aorta and the pulmonary artery as the left and right ventricles contract together.

Unlike the muscles in your leg or arm, which you can control at will, your heart muscle contracts whether you want it to or not. For this reason it is called involuntary muscle. This kind of muscle is also found in the walls of arteries, the vessels that take blood away from the heart and toward the tissues. The other major blood vessels, the veins, transport blood from the tissues toward the heart. In general the veins carry deoxygenated blood and the arteries carry oxygenated blood. The exception is the vessels that connect the heart and lungs. In this circuit the arteries carry deoxygenated blood and the veins carry oxygen-rich blood.

Muscle

Right ventricle

Chordae tendinae

Coronary arteries

Fat

Inferior vena cava

Lining

Outer coat

Muscular layer

Central channel

Elastic layer

Lining

Valve

The walls of an artery contain muscular layers which contract to move blood along every time the heart beats. Arteries do not have valves.

A vein has thinner walls than an artery and its central channel is larger. Veins have valves that prevent blood from flowing backwards.

Pulmonary artery

Branches of
pulmonary vein

Left atrium

Pulmonary valve

Mitral valve

Septum

A **single heartbeat** is
a complex process
in which the right and
left parts of the heart
work together.

Pulmonary veins

Right atrium

Left atrium

Ventricles

*The heart receives blood from
the body into the right atrium.
Blood that has been sent to
the lungs to pick up oxygen
returns and enters the heart
through the left atrium.*

A**n electrical** timing
system controls
the rate and directs the
sequence of heart
muscle contraction.

Aortic valve

Pulmonary valve

Tricuspid valve

Mitral valve

*At this point the tricuspid and
mitral valves open. the blood
moves down into the two
lower chambers, the
ventricles. The pulmonary and
aortic valves remain closed.*

T**he sounds** of a
heartbeat are called
lupp and dupp. They
are caused by the
different valves
slamming shut.

Aortic valve

Pulmonary valve

Tricuspid valve

Mitral valve

*Both ventricles are filled with
blood. The mitral and tricuspid
valves slam shut, causing the
first heart sound, the lupp,
which you can hear if you put
your ear to someone's chest.*

Aorta

Aortic valve

Pulmonary artery

Pulmonary valve

Right ventricle

T**he second** heart
sound, dupp, is
caused when the blood
has been pushed out of
the ventricles and the
pulmonary and aortic
valves slam shut.

Left ventricle

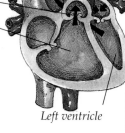

*The right ventricle contracts,
sending deoxygenated blood
on its circuit to the lungs. The
left ventricle contracts and
oxygenated blood is sent on
its way back to the body.*

Eye

Ear

Salivary gland

Muscle

Lymph nodes

Point where the
lymphatic system
joins the heart

Thymus gland

THE IMMUNE SYSTEM
THE BODY'S FIGHTING FORCE

YOUR BODY has an armed defense mechanism, the immune system, which it uses to repel invaders such as bacteria, viruses, and parasites. The immune system is complex, with many components. White blood cells are the body's fighting force. The bone marrow, thymus, lymph nodes, and spleen are sites of white cell production. The lymph system and the blood system transport white cells throughout the body.

The thymus gland of a child (below). The thymus is an important component of the immune system, producing a family of white blood cells called T cells. The thymus is large at birth and grows throughout childhood, but then shrinks. It is small in adults.

Heart

Spleen

The spleen is an organ that produces the B cells, which then mount an antibody response to invading organisms. It also acts as a recycling center, removing worn-out red and white cells from the body.

Areas of lymphatic tissue in the appendix and intestine, called Peyer's patches, are localized sites of B cell production.

Large intestine

Appendix

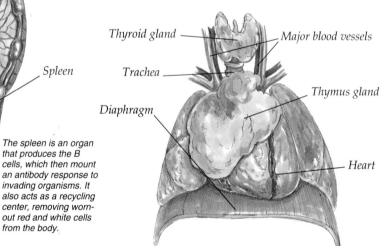

Thyroid gland

Major blood vessels

Trachea

Diaphragm

Thymus gland

Heart

The thymus gland is the site of production of different types of T cells. It produces killer T cells which can kill invading organisms or infected cells, by direct contact. Antigen-presenting T cells and memory cells are also made in the thymus. These work together to make sure that an immune response is mounted quickly when an infection takes place.

The lymph nodes, spleen, and bone marrow produce B cells which, in turn, produce antibodies.

C. SCRACE

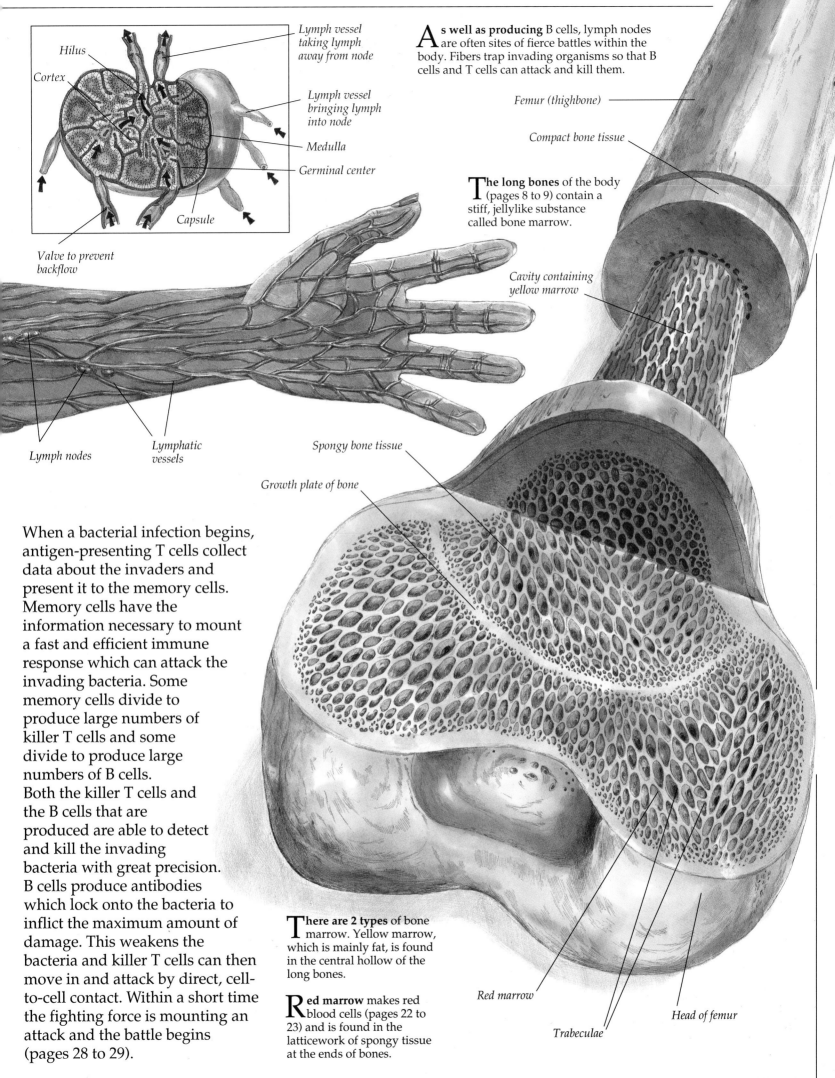

Hilus

Cortex

Lymph vessel taking lymph away from node

Lymph vessel bringing lymph into node

Medulla

Germinal center

Capsule

Valve to prevent backflow

Lymph nodes

Lymphatic vessels

As well as producing B cells, lymph nodes are often sites of fierce battles within the body. Fibers trap invading organisms so that B cells and T cells can attack and kill them.

Femur (thighbone)

Compact bone tissue

The long bones of the body (pages 8 to 9) contain a stiff, jellylike substance called bone marrow.

Cavity containing yellow marrow

Spongy bone tissue

Growth plate of bone

When a bacterial infection begins, antigen-presenting T cells collect data about the invaders and present it to the memory cells. Memory cells have the information necessary to mount a fast and efficient immune response which can attack the invading bacteria. Some memory cells divide to produce large numbers of killer T cells and some divide to produce large numbers of B cells.
Both the killer T cells and the B cells that are produced are able to detect and kill the invading bacteria with great precision. B cells produce antibodies which lock onto the bacteria to inflict the maximum amount of damage. This weakens the bacteria and killer T cells can then move in and attack by direct, cell-to-cell contact. Within a short time the fighting force is mounting an attack and the battle begins (pages 28 to 29).

There are 2 types of bone marrow. Yellow marrow, which is mainly fat, is found in the central hollow of the long bones.

Red marrow makes red blood cells (pages 22 to 23) and is found in the latticework of spongy tissue at the ends of bones.

Red marrow

Trabeculae

Head of femur

27

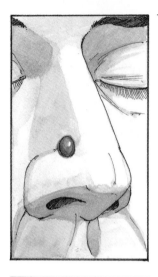

THE IMMUNE SYSTEM
THE BATTLE RAGES

Head of pimple

Pimple

Swollen tissue

EVERYONE HAS A PIMPLE now and then. It might not look too exciting from the outside, but inside, you could imagine that a medieval battle is raging! A pimple forms when bacteria invade the skin. They usually enter through a hair follicle and then damage the inside walls in an attempt to find a way into the rest of the body. The damage is soon noticed by antigen-presenting T cells which inform memory cells. The memory cells send killer T cells and B cells to the scene to attack the enemy.

A whitehead is a hair follicle that has become full of sebum, the oil which lubricates the outside of the skin.

A blackhead is more or less the same as a whitehead but its top has been oxidized by the air and turned black.

A pimple develops when the blocked hair follicle is invaded by bacteria. These cause damage to the hair follicle.

A boil is a very bad pimple. It is like a volcano in the skin. It is red and sore and is filled with yellow slime called pus.

If several hair follicles in the same patch of skin are infected this produces a boil with many heads: a carbuncle.

The Foot Soldiers are equipped with specially designed weapons that pierce and kill the invaders.

Blue Knight invaders, weakened by an attack by the Foot Soldiers' weapons, die when a Warrior Red Knight engages them in direct, hand-to-hand combat and inflicts piercing, fatal injuries.

*Pus containing
dead fighters*

The killer T cells fight invading
bacteria directly, by cell-to-cell
contact. B cells rush to the scene of
the battle and attack from a
distance by throwing antibodies at
the bacteria. The antibodies stick to
the surface of the invaders. Killer T
cells are attracted to bacteria which
have been attacked by antibodies.
They attack the weakened invaders
and quickly finish them off.

As the battle progresses the
number of dead bacteria and also
the number of white cell casualties
rise, and they and the battle debris
are taken away by macrophages.
Dead cells and fluid that cannot
be dealt with in this way are
released from the top of the pimple
as pus. Usually the battle ends in
victory for the body's fighting
force and within a few days
the pimple heals and
disappears.

Skin

Skin cells

The Blue Knights represent
the invading bacteria.

The Chief Warriors
represent the memory cells.

The Warrior Red Knights
represent the killer T cells.

The Foot Soldiers represent
B cells. Their weapons
represent antibodies.

The Debris Collectors
represent macrophages.

Scouts represent antigen-
presenting T cells.

The huge influx of
fighters into the
skin causes a swelling.
This is seen as a lump
on the surface.

Debris Collectors
collect the dead
from the battlefield
and take them away
for disposal.

When the number
of dead becomes
too great to clear away
they are forced out of
the pimple as pus.

LOOKING AT THE BODY
THE BODY IN ACTION

THE HUMAN BODY is a complicated and intricate machine and it is a masterpiece of engineering. The bones of the body form its supporting framework. Muscles and bones work together at joints to give movement in different directions. Large muscles give the body its strength for lifting and pushing, while small muscles allow fine movements. Elastic but tough ligaments link muscles to bones and give flexibility for bending and stretching.

Moving outside the body's natural limits has its risks. Some early balloonists died from lack of oxygen when they drifted too high into the air and lost consciousness.

A cyclist propels himself forward using strong leg muscles to flex and extend his legs at the ankle, knee, and hip joints.

The spine is flexible; it allows us to bend forward, backward, and sideways.

Housework involves stretching and bending using the bones and muscles in the spine.

Ironing a shirt uses the shoulder, elbow, wrist, and finger joints. Movements of the arm muscles are co-ordinated by the brain, using data collected by the eyes.

The muscles of circus strongman acts (above left) and bodybuilders (above right) are huge because of diet and training. These athletes eat a lot of protein to provide their body with the material it needs to build muscle tissue. They then exercise with weights to develop large and obvious muscles.

You are not born with the ability to move in a coordinated way. A newborn baby has some reflex actions: sucking, grasping, and flinging its arms wide when surprised. But it has to learn to sit up, crawl, and then walk. Once the movements of walking have been learned they become automatic, and faster movements like running, skipping, and dancing become possible.

You need strong arm and leg muscles and flexible knee, shoulder, and elbow joints to dig a garden well.

A man climbing a ladder uses the muscles and joints in both of his arms and legs. His eyes and inner ears enable him to balance.

A smooching couple uses data from body contact to time dance movements.

Standing on a moving horse needs fine control of the feet and leg muscles. This athlete's sense of balance has been developed by years of practice.

Ballroom dancing is a fun social activity which helps to keep the leg muscles in good condition.

Good hand, eye, and brain coordination is necessary for typing. Experts can type as many as 100 words a minute.

The body can adjust to new environments well into adult life. Climbers make more red blood cells to compensate for the lack of oxygen in the high mountains. Astronauts' leg muscles become weak when they have been in space, but training can make them strong again on return to Earth.

Sky divers develop strong arm muscles to control the movement of their parachutes and use keen eyesight to pick out their landing targets.

Trapeze artists can perform daring feats of exceptional balance and muscle control.

Running or jogging regularly strengthens the muscles in the heart and makes the lungs more efficient. Running too often on hard roads can cause damage to the hip and knee joints.

Walking on stilts (left) or dancing in a ballet (right) are entertaining to watch but not easy to do. Stilt walking needs good balance and the ability to fall properly. Ballet dancers build up strong muscles in their feet as they often put all their weight onto their toes.

Astronauts move slowly and clumsily in their protective suits.

Many astronauts are sick until they get used to being weightless.

Gymnasts have supple muscles and flexible joints.

Circus performers such as fire-eaters (right) and escape artists (left) use strong muscles and good coordination to convince their audience that they are witnessing amazing feats.

A jazz saxophonist has agile hand muscles and flexible finger joints.

A cowboy on a bronco uses his strong thigh muscles to clamp his thighs and knees to the body of the horse.

Swimmers usually have large shoulder muscles.

A window washer uses his arms and shoulder joints and a good sense of balance to clean windows from the top of a ladder.

Juggling involves good coordination between the eyes and the muscles in the arms and hands.

Opera singers have muscular diaphragms and well-developed muscles between their ribs. This enables them to control their breathing and to sing with great power.

Soccer players can run fast and have good control of their foot movements for dribbling.

Skipping develops strong calf muscles.

Many people say that 1 hour of sleep before midnight is worth 2 hours after midnight. This might be true. Body temperature and metabolism decrease in the evening, and rise in the morning.

If we force the body to stay awake when it wants to sleep, and make it sleep when it is ready for activity, our normal sleep patterns are disrupted and we can become tired and irritable.

Eye movements usually accompany dreaming. This period of sleep is called Rapid Eye Movement (REM) sleep. If woken just after REM sleep, people remember their dream.

During the night Mr. and Mrs. Rogers will sleep through the 4 different stages of sleep in several cycles, each lasting 80 to 120 minutes. They each wake up 4 times and have about 7 dreams.

We all have a built-in daily rhythm that directs our sleeping habits. Experiments that study people's natural daily rhythms without reference to clocks or clues from daylight show that many people do not have an exact 24-hour rhythm. They automatically sleep and wake according to their internal clock, which is 2 or 3 hours shorter, or longer, than 24 hours.

At midnight Mr. and Mrs. Rogers are both in stage 3 sleep.

When Mr. and Mrs. Rogers settle down for a typical night's sleep, they relax and then start drowsing. During drowsing, the movements of their limbs and eyes are under voluntary control. They produce the type of brain waves which show they are relaxed with their eyes shut.

After an hour and a half they feel very sleepy and turn out the light just before 11 p.m.

Many adults experience sleep problems. Anxiety and depression can cause insomnia, the inability to sleep well. Taking care of a baby can disturb parents' sleep patterns for years afterward. The opposite of insomnia, hypersomnia, leads to excessive sleeping. Sufferers sleep for 18–20 hours a day and can collapse into a sleeplike state when under stress.

LOOKING AT THE BODY
THE BODY AT REST

SLEEP AND REST are important for your body's health and well-being. We spend a third of our lives asleep but we do not really understand why we need to sleep. Some experts think that the body needs to shut down for a few hours each day so that body repair and maintenance can take place. Some think that dreaming is the body's way of rerunning events of the day in order to retain memories.

At 9 p.m. Mr. and Mrs. Rogers decide to have an early night and go to bed with a hot drink and a good book.

As the body enters the first stage of sleep, breathing becomes more even and eye movements become slow and rolling. Brainwaves lengthen and wave patterns typical of sleep appear.

The second stage of sleep is called REM, or light sleep. This is the stage which is most common during a night's sleep, in old and young people. Dreaming occurs during this stage.

We all dream for a few minutes, 4 or 5 times every night. Often the dreams are not remembered. Those which are usually occur just before waking. During a dream, most of the muscles of the body, except for the eyes and respiratory system, are paralyzed. Breathing and heart rate increase and the eyes often move rapidly, from side to side, under the closed lids.

The amount of sleep that people need depends on their lifestyle and their age. Eight hours is average for a young adult with a reasonably active lifestyle. A newborn baby sleeps for sixteen hours a day, an adolescent often sleeps for ten to twelve hours when he or she is growing rapidly, and a person of seventy-five may need only four or five hours.

Four different stages of sleep occur during the night. During stage one we doze, and this leads into the second stage, a period of light sleep when we are most likely to dream. Two stages of deep sleep follow and the body becomes totally limp and relaxed. We travel through the different stages several times each night and often wake up two or three times.

By 3 a.m. Mr. Rogers has had 2 vivid dreams in REM sleep while Mrs. Rogers has had a long period of stage 3 sleep.

At 4 a.m. Mrs. Rogers is dreaming and Mr. Rogers is in the middle of stage 4 sleep.

People who sleep for 7 to 9 hours each night live longer than those who sleep more, or less, than this average.

When deprived of sleep for only 2 or 3 days, most people become distressed. The balance of vital chemicals in the brain becomes upset and stress hormones are secreted into the blood by the adrenal glands. Physical and mental skills are lost, and a chemical builds up which causes hallucinations. Lack of sleep can cause death faster than lack of food.

Alcohol may help people to fall asleep but then it acts as a stimulant, waking them up in the early hours of the morning.

At 5 a.m. Mr. Rogers' bladder sends signals to his brain to tell him that it is full of urine.

Someone who drinks lots of coffee during the day may find that the caffeine makes it difficult for him or her to get to sleep.

The brainwave patterns of stage 2 sleep show faster waves than those seen in stage 1. Distinctive patterns, called spindles and saw-toothed waves, occur just before dreaming.

Stage 3 sleep is a deep and restful sleep. The muscles relax completely and the heart rate falls. Blood pressure drops and breathing slows. There is no eye movement.

Brainwaves of great height and depth are recorded during this stage of sleep. Most people experience stage 3 sleep later in the night but not in the first few hours after they fall asleep.

Stage 4 sleep, the deepest sleep of all, can occur after stage 3 sleep or right after stage 2. Early in the night a jump from stage 2 to 4 is more likely. Later, stage 3 sleep appears.

During stage 4 sleep, the brainwaves are high and wide. Heart rate and blood pressure reach their lowest points. There are no eye movements and muscular activity is very low.

The pituitary gland releases growth hormone during this stage of sleep and this is thought to explain why babies spend most of their sleeping time in the stages of deep sleep.

CARING FOR THE BODY
BODY MAINTENANCE

The illustration on the far right shows the types of food that you should eat every day to keep healthy and fit. The illustration on the right shows foods that are high in fat and sugar. These are not very good for you and you should avoid eating them too often.

YOUR BODY IS A COMPLEX MACHINE. Like most machines, it needs regular maintenance to keep it in good working order. You need to feed the body with suitable fuel, exercise regularly to keep joints and muscles supple and strong, and avoid poisons and pollutants which can affect the body's performance. The outside of the body must be kept clean and groomed to avoid acne and blemishes.

Control room (brain)

Dirt and bacteria must be removed from his skin, especially from the areas under his arms.

Robotman's skull contains his body's control room. This is manned by engineers who direct the actions of the body. They look for signs of damage or injury and send out teams of workers to make repairs. The waterproof skin covering has to be cleaned each day to stop grime from building up and affecting the delicate sense organs on the face. In dry conditions it needs to be oiled to avoid cracking. The teeth and mouth, the point of entry for robotman's fuel, must be kept clear of debris.

Food inlet (mouth)

Series of flexible back hinges (vertebrae)

Eating the right kinds of food provides the body with the correct fuel. Protein, from meat, fish, dairy products, or legumes and grains, is used to build muscles and repair tissue. Carbohydrate from fruit, grains, and cereals gives the body energy. Vitamins and minerals from all kinds of foods provide the raw materials to maintain the complex processes which make the body work.

The right kind of fuel is needed to keep the main engine room and all the moving parts in good order.

The main pump room circulates oxygen and fuel to all the moving parts. It is hidden from view by the metal body casing (rib cage).

Hinges (joints)

Electronic circuits (nerves)

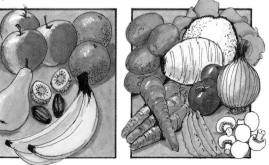

Eating fresh fruit and vegetables gives your body many of the vitamins it needs to be healthy. Oranges contain vitamin C, carrots contain vitamin A, and green vegetables contain the B vitamins and vitamin K.

As well as being a source of protein, fish also provides vitamin A, vitamin D, calcium, and iron.

Fresh meat and dairy products are high in protein and in fat. They should not be eaten to excess.

Heavy drinking of alcohol over several years can lead to serious liver disease. Also, the high number of calories in alcoholic drinks can lead to regular drinkers becoming overweight.

Although not smoking at all is the only option for someone who wants to be healthy, adults can enjoy alcohol in moderation, with no ill effects.

Smoking leads to a higher risk of lung cancer and heart disease. Even one cigarette a day may cause a smoker to die earlier than he or she might have.

Sports and exercise are important components of a healthy lifestyle. It is a good idea to exercise for half an hour, at least three times every week.

Exercise is particularly important for young people. Running, jumping, and playing sports helps the body to become strong and improves coordination.

Eating a balanced diet is one of the keys to good health. Many experts believe that eating plenty of fresh food is better than always relying on highly processed foods.

Exercise and hygiene are important in body maintenance. Taking part in a sport or activity which significantly increases your heart rate for 20–30 minutes at least three times a week is a good way to keep healthy. It helps your limbs move smoothly, your muscles stay firm and strong, and your heart and lungs to work well. Regular exercise also makes you feel good mentally; you lose feelings of tension and you sleep more deeply.

Regular washing or showering removes the sweat and grime that build up during the course of the day, and keeps your skin and scalp free from infection. Washing your hands carefully after using the bathroom keeps you from spreading bacteria which may cause stomach upsets. Brushing your teeth after eating and last thing at night removes plaque from teeth and prevents decay.

Muscles that are working hard must be checked for signs of damage and repaired quickly.

Robotman's joints must be kept lubricated to avoid wear and tear as he moves.

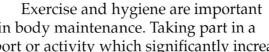

Mid-leg hinge (knee joint)

Metal framework (bony skeleton)

Main hinge between body and legs (pelvis and hip joints)

Every day, robotman is shut down for a few hours so that the maintenance engineers can complete all repairs.

Hydraulic piston (muscles)

Tubes carrying water, oxygen, and fuel (arteries and veins)

The body of this giant robotman, with his skeleton of steel, his complex electronic circuits, and his waterproof skin, illustrates the different ways in which the human body needs to be maintained in order to stay healthy.

Legumes and grains are low in fat. Eaten together, they provide a good source of protein.

Aerobics and weight training increase fitness generally and make the muscles firmer.

Running regularly builds up general body stamina and fitness as well as strong leg muscles.

Racing cyclists have strong hearts and healthy lungs. Their legs have well-developed muscles.

Swimming is a good form of exercise because it tones all the muscles in the body.

Brisk, regular walking makes the heart and lungs stronger and also builds up leg muscles.

CARING FOR THE BODY
THE POLLUTED BODY

SMOKING CIGARETTES and drinking large amounts of alcohol can seriously damage the body's health. Smoking just a few cigarettes a day reduces lung efficiency. Breathing becomes harder and most smokers develop a cough. People who smoke over a long period of time run a much higher risk of lung diseases such as emphysema (when the air sacs in the lungs are destroyed and the lungs become overexpanded and inefficient), repeated attacks of bronchitis, and cancer. Smoking also affects the heart and blood vessels; many smokers suffer from raised, or high, blood pressure.

People find it hard to stop smoking because the nicotine in cigarettes is addictive. Giving up smoking results in withdrawal symptoms such as irritability, headaches, and stomach pains.

Smoking during pregnancy is very dangerous. Babies born to women who smoke are much more likely to be underweight at birth.

The clothes of smokers smell of smoke, as do their homes.

The hair and fingers of a smoker may become tinged with yellow color because of the effect of nicotine.

Blood clots are more common in smokers and these can cause strokes and heart attacks.

Smokers sometimes inflict their smoke on other people. One person dies every day from the effects of passive smoking.

Smokers usually have bad breath and their teeth can become yellow.

Heart

Lungs

Smokers often get premature wrinkles around their mouth and eyes. These are caused by the drying effects of the smoke and because smokers scrunch up their faces when inhaling.

Abdomen

Smoking can contribute to the development of an ulcer as well as abdominal discomfort and heartburn.

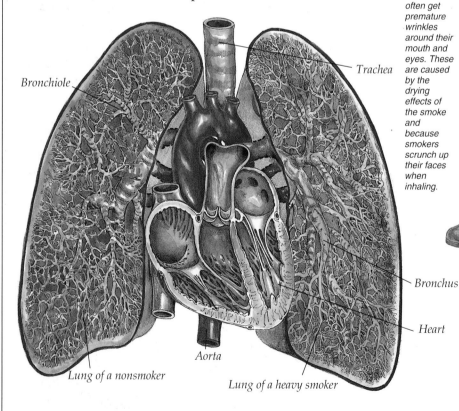

Bronchiole

Trachea

Bronchus

Heart

Aorta

Lung of a nonsmoker

Lung of a heavy smoker

Nicotine makes the blood vessels narrower and this leads to varicose veins.

Veins

The effects of nicotine lead to bad circulation in the feet.

A nonsmoking adult has lungs that look like the one on the left. The lungs of a smoker become like the one on the right. The smoke and tar from the cigarettes discolor the lung tissue. As they are damaged, the lungs become prone to infection.

Nicotine causes small blood vessels in the smoker's body to constrict (get narrow). The smoker's heart has to work harder to push blood through them and it becomes enlarged. The normal heart shown above would be larger in a heavy smoker with secondary heart disease.

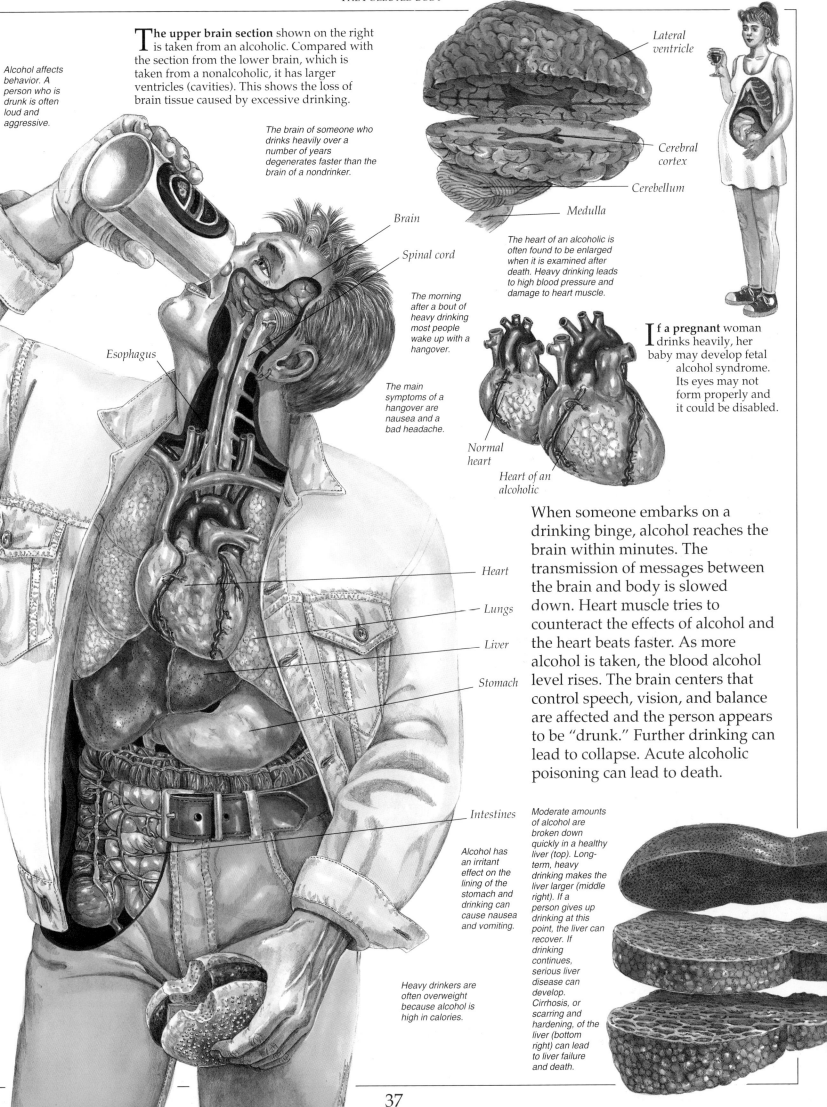

The upper brain section shown on the right is taken from an alcoholic. Compared with the section from the lower brain, which is taken from a nonalcoholic, it has larger ventricles (cavities). This shows the loss of brain tissue caused by excessive drinking.

Alcohol affects behavior. A person who is drunk is often loud and aggressive.

The brain of someone who drinks heavily over a number of years degenerates faster than the brain of a nondrinker.

Lateral ventricle

Cerebral cortex

Cerebellum

Medulla

Brain

Spinal cord

Esophagus

The morning after a bout of heavy drinking most people wake up with a hangover.

The main symptoms of a hangover are nausea and a bad headache.

The heart of an alcoholic is often found to be enlarged when it is examined after death. Heavy drinking leads to high blood pressure and damage to heart muscle.

Normal heart

Heart of an alcoholic

If a pregnant woman drinks heavily, her baby may develop fetal alcohol syndrome. Its eyes may not form properly and it could be disabled.

Heart

Lungs

Liver

Stomach

When someone embarks on a drinking binge, alcohol reaches the brain within minutes. The transmission of messages between the brain and body is slowed down. Heart muscle tries to counteract the effects of alcohol and the heart beats faster. As more alcohol is taken, the blood alcohol level rises. The brain centers that control speech, vision, and balance are affected and the person appears to be "drunk." Further drinking can lead to collapse. Acute alcoholic poisoning can lead to death.

Intestines

Alcohol has an irritant effect on the lining of the stomach and drinking can cause nausea and vomiting.

Heavy drinkers are often overweight because alcohol is high in calories.

Moderate amounts of alcohol are broken down quickly in a healthy liver (top). Long-term, heavy drinking makes the liver larger (middle right). If a person gives up drinking at this point, the liver can recover. If drinking continues, serious liver disease can develop. Cirrhosis, or scarring and hardening, of the liver (bottom right) can lead to liver failure and death.

WHEN THE BODY FAILS
THE DAMAGED BODY

Your BODY CAN HEAL AND REPAIR ITSELF efficiently, but sometimes the damage caused by injury or illness is too great for the body to cope with. Modern medical technology can now help the body recover from traumas which, only a few years ago, would have been fatal or totally disabling. Hands, noses, ears, lower arms and legs, feet, toes, and fingers, severed in an accident, can all now be rejoined to the body using microsurgery. More people who suffer heart attacks can now be helped by new drugs, heart bypass operations, and intensive care. Someone with a very badly damaged heart can even be given new valves or a pacemaker, or sometimes, a completely new heart. Broken bones can be expertly set and surgery can pin and screw broken pieces of bone into place so that they can heal effectively.

Ulna

Radius

Tendons

Vein

Skin

Radial artery

Blood

Microsurgery enables part of the body to be sewn back into place after accidental amputation.

A hand that is severed cleanly is much easier to restore than one which has also been crushed and damaged.

An operation to sew back a severed hand takes about eight hours.

The severed hand is put into a dry polyethylene bag. It is then placed into a bowl of ice. Several layers of gauze protect the hand from direct contact with the ice.

The severed hand is transported to the hospital with its owner, whose arm has been tied with a tourniquet to stop the bleeding, and then loosely bandaged.

On arrival at the hospital the patient is rushed to the operating room to be anesthetized and prepared for the complex operation to sew back the severed hand.

The first priority is to restore blood flow to the hand by joining the ends of the arteries together. The stitching must be tight to stop blood from leaking out.

The two main bones of the arm are then joined together, often by using metal plates to hold them properly in position so that healing can take place.

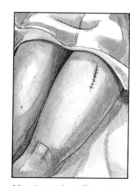

Muscle, tendons, ligaments, and bone can be taken from other parts of the body and used to reconstruct tissue in the hand or wrist that has been too severely damaged.

Once blood vessels and bones have been rejoined, delicate stitching is used to sew together the muscles which will give the hand the chance to regain movement.

After the operation, several months of physiotherapy are needed. Rejoined nerves do not grow back very easily and this makes healing and general progress slow.

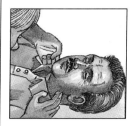
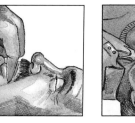

When someone collapses with a heart attack a qualified first-aider checks to see if he or she is still breathing.

If not, the first-aider uses a finger to explore the victim's mouth, making sure that the airways are clear.

The head of the heart attack patient is then tilted back and the first-aider gives artificial respiration.

If the heart stops, the first-aider must administer cardiopulmonary resuscitation, or CPR, which keeps the brain supplied with oxygen. The first-aider presses down on the victim's chest on the breastbone 15 times and then gives two slow, mouth-to-mouth breaths.

This should get the person breathing again and restart the heart. The ambulance should arrive soon.

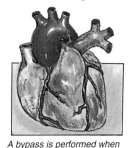
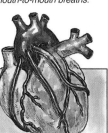

Trained paramedics take over and the patient is rushed to the emergency room of the local hospital.

A heart attack happens when the arteries that supply the heart muscle with oxygenated blood become blocked and heart muscle dies. Doctors can now help some heart attack victims by carrying out a coronary artery bypass operation.

A bypass is performed when the coronary artery is blocked and cannot supply blood to a large part of the heart.

The operation adds new blood vessels, taken from other parts of the body, to "bypass" the damage.

After several days in intensive care the patient can begin to convalesce. Many make a full recovery.

There are several different types of fracture. In a compound fracture the jagged edges of the broken bone stick out of the skin. In a simple fracture, the bone remains inside the body.

Fractures heal more quickly in children because their bones are more supple than an adult's. A broken thighbone in a baby heals in three weeks, but in a twenty-year-old takes about five months.

Children often have greenstick fractures, where the bone is broken on one side and bent on the other.

A broken bone is called a fracture. Some fractured bones – ribs, for example – heal naturally, without medical attention, but most long bones need a plaster cast. This keeps the two ends of the fracture together and holds them still so that natural healing processes can take place. In very severe fractures where the bone is broken in several places, metal plates may be screwed into the bone to give it extra strength.

Within a few days of the broken limb being encased in its cast, a callus forms in the gap between the bones. After a week new bone tissue begins to grow and knits the ends of the bones together. Cartilage is deposited in the outer collar around the break and this is replaced by new bone over a number of weeks. Usually the only remaining sign of a simple fracture is a bump on the bone at the point where the break occurred.

In an incomplete fracture the bone cracks but does not break apart.

In a complete fracture the bone breaks into two separate pieces.

In old people, bones break very easily. Sometimes a hipbone breaks under the strain of walking.

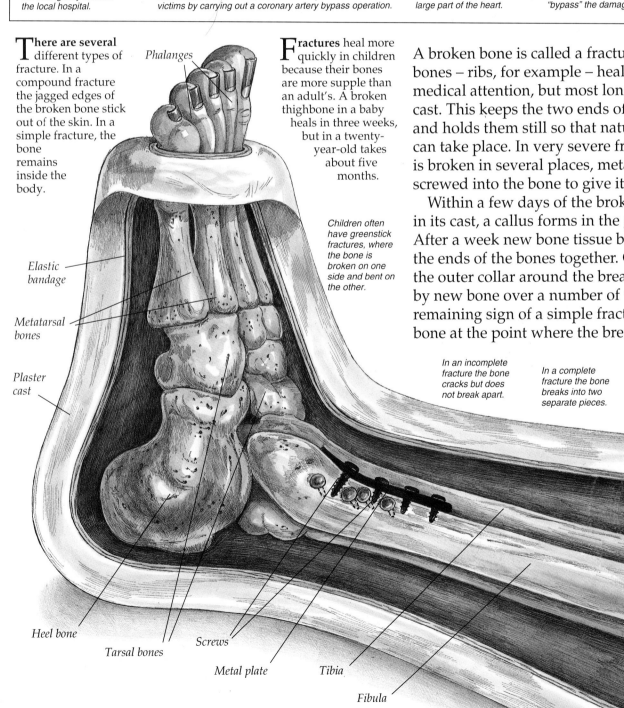

Phalanges

Elastic bandage

Metatarsal bones

Plaster cast

Heel bone

Tarsal bones

Screws

Metal plate

Tibia

Fibula

26652

The main threats to life change with age. Accidents kill most of the young adults who die each year. Middle-aged women run a high risk of cancer, for example breast cancer; men run a high risk of heart disease. In the over-70s the big killers of both men and women are heart disease, cancer, and lung disease.

WHEN THE BODY FAILS
GROWING OLD

MANY OF YOUR BODY'S FUNCTIONS reach their peak during young adulthood. After the age of thirty the body continues to change and develop, but the changes generally result in loss of function. An average person in a western country like the United States, who has good living conditions and eats a healthy, balanced diet, exercises, and is sensible about smoking and drinking (pages 34 to 37), can live to be eighty or even older.

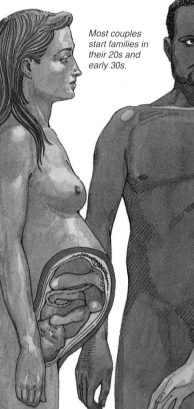

Twenty-five year olds need to sleep for 7 to 8 hours each night.

Changes in the inner ear mean that you become less susceptible to motion sickness after the age of 20.

A woman is most fertile at the age of 28. Over 85% of her monthly cycles result in a fertile egg.

Most couples start families in their 20s and early 30s.

After the age of 20, women have a higher proportion of fat in their bodies compared to men.

The over-40s need to sleep for 6 to 7 hours each night.

At 25 a man's body is 24% lean body mass (muscle, nerves, or bone), 16% fat and 60% water.

A woman's body is 22.5% lean body mass, 22.5% fat, and 55% water.

At the age of 40 a man's body is made up of 21% lean body mass, 19% fat, and 60% water.

A woman's body is 19.5% lean body mass, 25.5% fat, and 55% water.

Men can build up muscle tissue more easily than women.

From about your 30th birthday your body begins to shrink at the rate of ½ inch (1 cm) every 10 years.

The liver and kidneys lose one third of their weight between the ages of 30 and 90.

By the age of 40 the hair starts to turn gray as pigment cells in the scalp lose their activity.

The skin becomes thinner and wrinkles become obvious in exposed areas such as the face.

At 50, many people experience "middle age spread," putting on weight around the abdomen.

Many women cannot give birth after the age of 50 but many men have fertile sperm at 70.

From the age of 40 the heart becomes less flexible. Elasticity in the arteries decreases and the blood vessels become more rigid. The coronary arteries can harden or become blocked, and heart attacks become more common.

Enamel is lost from the teeth, and the gums recede. Tooth decay is difficult to avoid and many adults eventually need dentures. The cells lining the mouth divide more slowly in the elderly and mouth sores take longer to heal.

Between 50 and 70, the reflexes slow and reaction time increases. The ability to feel heat and pain decreases. In the very old, pain from an injury is felt more sharply because the thinning skin exposes nerve endings.

Your body begins to function less efficiently after about the age of forty. Women find it more difficult to become pregnant at forty-five: only 40% of their monthly cycles result in fertile eggs, compared to over 85% at the age of twenty-eight. There is also a much greater risk of giving birth to a child with Down Syndrome after the age of forty. Men and women start to lose muscle fibers, kidney tissue, and tissue from bone marrow. The senses of sight, hearing, and taste become less acute. The weight of the brain decreases after the age of twenty-five and cells are lost from the cerebral cortex. The risk of dying increases with age. At twenty, seven men in every 1,000 die every year; by sixty, 193 in every 1,000 die every year; and 500 in every 1,000 men over the age of seventy die every year.

Many men go bald in middle age because hair follicles on the scalp die.

The immune system becomes less efficient and older people are more likely to get infections and more serious illnesses like cancer.

Improved medical technology means that more people now live to be older. Many of the diseases that killed young people in the past – such as smallpox, measles, and other infections – can now be prevented. Diseases common in older people, such as arthritis and cancer, can be treated more successfully, increasing the quantity and quality of life of the elderly.

The heart valves stiffen with age.

The cornea of the eye becomes thinner after middle age.

Lung tissue becomes less elastic.

People over 70 need to sleep for 4 or 5 hours each night.

Fingernails and toenails grow more slowly.

Calcium deposits in the nails turn them yellow.

The body loses muscle tissue and gains connective tissue.

At the age of 65, men are 18% lean body mass, 24% fat, and 58% water.

Women are 15% lean body mass, 28% fat, and 54% water.

Bones become more brittle and break easily.

The ability to hear high-frequency sounds decreases and the sense of smell declines after 60.

After the age of 65, red blood cells become more fragile and their numbers decrease.

Taste buds die and are not replaced. By the age of 70 only 70% of those present at 20 are still active.

Bone loses minerals as it ages. It becomes thinner and weaker and fractures more easily.

By the age of 80 the joints shrink and foot arches flatten. The spine curves more as spinal disks wither.

Muscle mass decreases with age: it reduces by 30% between the ages of 30 and 80.

THE BODY THROUGH THE AGES

THE CUSTOMIZED BODY
THE BODY THROUGH THE AGES

HUMAN BEINGS ARE DESCENDED from bipedal mammals which evolved from the ape family. Early manlike apes first appeared in Africa around 5,000,000 B.C. They gathered fruit and other plants for food and lived in the open, rather than in trees like their ape ancestors. After over four million years of evolution, human beings similar to ourselves began to emerge. They lived in groups, gathered fruit and plants, and hunted animals for meat. They could make tools and weapons, build shelters, and make fire. Their large brains enabled them to develop language, and complex civilizations began to emerge from about 3,500 B.C.

As humans developed from their bipedal apelike ancestors they became taller and adopted a more upright stance. Their larger brains enabled them to have greater intelligence and to develop complex social behavior.

The Vikings extended their territory throughout northern Europe between A.D. 800 and 1000. They had hard lives, and skeletons found at Hedeby show that Viking women lived to be about 24 years old, on average.

Queen Elizabeth I set trends with her white face and shaved eyebrows and hairline. Newly discovered sugar rotted her teeth and the lead-based face paint destroyed her skin.

Knights from the Middle Ages are commonly thought of as being very short. Experts now think that they were only about 2 inches (5 cm) shorter, on average, than a male adult of today. Men today reach the same height as Stone Age men.

The Elizabethans thought that bathing could damage their bodies. Some are said to have been washed only 3 times – when they were born, when they were married, and when they died. Between baths, they disguised stale smells by carrying posies of flowers and herbs.

During World War II (1939–1945) surgeons developed plastic surgery to help badly burned airmen.

In the 1920s and 1930s the depression hit Europe and America. Poverty was very common and many people struggled to feed their families.

In 1930s' America, gangsters controlled large sections of society. Alcohol was banned but people distilled it illegally.

In the 1940s antibiotics were developed and free medical care became available in Britain as the National Health Service was set up in 1948. As an escape from poor living conditions, American communities such as in Detroit developed jazz and blues music.

In World War I (1914–1918) field hospitals were used to help soldiers wounded in the terrible battles in the trenches. Over 8.7 million people were killed in this war.

The ancient Egyptians (below) had their bodies preserved after death in a process called mummification.

The Minoans (3000–1500 B.C.) formed an early European civilization. Men and women used tight corsets made with animal bones to bind their waists.

The ancient Greeks (right) excelled at sports, and were physically very fit. They had great intelligence and developed sophisticated architecture.

The Romans (right) also had a highly developed civilization with a great empire that stretched over much of the world. They are famous for their high standards of hygiene and their advanced water supply systems. They used oil to remove dirt from their bodies and bathed regularly in clean, hot water.

Until recently the Japanese had a tradition of binding the feet of young girls. This was done to make them walk delicately, but also meant that their feet could not grow properly.

Early American Indians (c. 1000 B.C.), smeared red ocher clay onto their bodies. It had antibacterial properties and acted as a primitive deodorant.

The Australian aborigines were hunter-gatherers who knew their rough environment intimately.

Primitive man had a much shorter life span than we have today. Two hundred years ago, people could only expect to live for thirty years. By the 1800s, life expectancy had increased to fifty years, and today people in the western world have a life expectancy of about eighty years. This dramatic change has resulted from the great improvements in living conditions that have occurred, and the advances in medical technology and care which have been made since 1800.

In the late 1950s the birthrate in Britain and the United States peaked in a period known as the "baby boom." By 1960, 22 percent of the population was under ten years old. This was nearly 6 percent more than normal. The total population of the United States rose by 80 million between 1940 and 1974.

Victorian women's corsets were so tight that they often caused their wearers to faint.

Today fitness and health are of great importance (right). Many people keep their bodies fit by exercising regularly and by eating a healthy diet. They do not smoke and limit their alcohol intake to a safe level; fourteen units per week for women, and twenty-one for men.

The 1950s saw the beginning of the influence of television on the lives of people in the western world.

In the 1960s (above) and the 1970s (right) young people rejected the traditional values of society and dressed and behaved to make a statement.

Fashions became more outrageous in the 1980s and tattooing, body painting and piercing were practiced.

THE CUSTOMIZED BODY
THE PERFECT BODY?

ALL HUMAN BODIES are similar, but not identical. Individuals in the same family may differ in hair and eye color and body size and shape. Worldwide, there are many races with different skin colors and distinctive facial features. People from most races and civilizations have tried to accentuate their individuality by changing their appearance.

Some Indian and African tribes still practice traditional methods of body decoration, according to customs and religious ceremonies. The most common forms of body decoration include coloring the skin, wearing elaborate jewelry to distort parts of the body, and scarring the body to produce skin patterns. Decoration is done to attract members of the opposite sex, to show the status of a person within a tribe, or to show aggression.

Women from Mauritania decorate their hands and feet with intricate patterns using henna. The patterns draw attention to their movements as they dance a ritual dance of love for the men in their villages.

In tattooing the dye is injected into the skin and cannot be easily removed.

Scarification, cutting patterns in the skin, is a common way for African women to decorate their bodies. The cuts heal over, but raised scars remain on the body as elaborate and long-lasting patterns.

Women of the Mondari tribe, from a Sudanese village south of Tali Post, have cropped hair and scarification patterns around the forehead. The star-shaped scar around the navel dates from a beauty ceremony performed at puberty.

Elaborate gold jewelry, pendants, beads, neck chains, earrings, and a headband are used by this married woman of the Masai tribe in Kenya. Her enormous earrings weigh about 1 lb (0.5 kg) each.

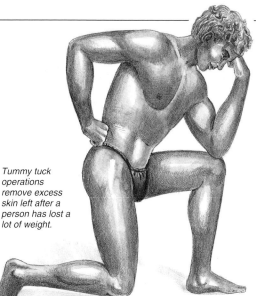

Tummy tuck operations remove excess skin left after a person has lost a lot of weight.

Baldness can now be treated by an operation to implant hair, taken from other parts of the body, into the scalp.

Face-lifts, cheek implants, and chin enlargements are done to make a person look younger.

Collagen injections into the lips make them larger and thicker. This is not permanent, as the collagen is absorbed by the body.

Cosmetic surgery to change the shape of the nose is now a routine operation.

Surgery to change the shape and size of the breasts is usually done for women, but breast implants for men who want a more muscular chest without exercising are now available.

In more technologically advanced societies, body decoration and manipulation are also common. Many women wear makeup and men and women use clothes and jewelry to show their individuality and social status. They can also change the shape of their bodies by using special diets and by exercising with weights. More drastically, some change their bodies by cosmetic surgery. Although this type of surgery is more common for women, more operations have recently become available for men. A man who wants to change his appearance completely can do so with at least seventeen different operations.

The Erigpactsa Indians live along the banks of the Juruena River in Brazil. The body decorations of this chief are a sign of his skill as a warrior.

The nose plumes of the Erigpactsa chief pierce the soft tissue between his nostrils. The skin of his earlobes has been stretched by wooden disks.

Women of the Ndebele people of South Africa wear metal rings called iindzila around their necks. The weight of the rings increases the distance between the neck vertebrae and pushes down the collarbones.

Iindzila

Neck vertebrae

Sternum

Clavicle (collarbone)

Rib cage

This fierce warrior of the Suya tribe from Brazil has a wooden disk inserted between his lower gums and lip.

A Hindu from Malaysia is pierced by needles and hooks during the religious ceremony of Thaipusam. He is in a trance and seems to feel no pain.

GLOSSARY

Antibody One of a family of protein molecules that are produced by B cells. Antibodies attach to the surface of bacteria and other pathogens and weaken them.

Antigen A substance against which an antibody is produced.

Antigen-presenting T cell A white blood cell which is a component of the immune system. It presents fragments (antigens) of invading organisms to other cells in the immune system so that they can prepare to defend the body.

Aorta The largest artery in the body. It carries oxygenated blood, pumped from the left ventricle, out toward the body tissue.

Appendix A narrow, finger-shaped piece of the large intestine which has no apparent function.

Artery Blood vessel that carries oxygenated blood from the heart to the body. Only the pulmonary artery carries deoxygenated blood.

Atrium The left and right atria are the two smaller chambers at the top of the heart. They pump blood down to the ventricles.

Autonomic nervous system The part of the nervous system that controls automatic functions, such as heartbeat and sweating.

Bacteria Small, single-celled organisms, some of which cause illness when they invade the body.

B cell A type of white blood cell which is part of the immune system. It produces antibodies.

Bladder A thin-walled, muscular sac that stores urine until it can be released from the body.

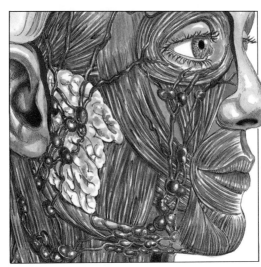

Bone marrow The soft material found in some bones. Yellow marrow is found in the central cavity of long bones. Red marrow is found in the honeycomb structure at the ends of long bones.

Brain stem Part of the brain that links the spinal cord with the other parts of the brain.

Capillaries The tiny blood vessels that are the furthest from the heart. They connect the ends of the arteries with the ends of the veins.

Cartilage A type of connective tissue that provides support and aids movement at joints.

Cerebellum Part of the brain found underneath the cerebrum, at the back of the skull.

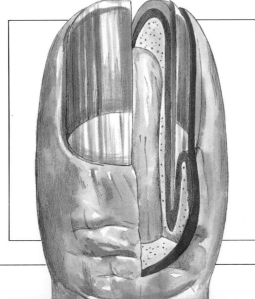

Cerebrum The largest and most highly developed part of the brain.

Cervix The neck of the uterus. It dilates (opens) during labor to allow the birth of the baby.

Cirrhosis A serious liver disease in which liver cells are destroyed and then replaced by abnormal fatty tissue. It leads to liver failure.

Colostrum A fluid, high in protein and antibodies, released from a mother's breasts during the first three days after she has given birth.

Conception The fertilization of an egg by a sperm, leading to the development of an embryo.

Digestion The chemical conversion of large food particles into small, absorbable molecules.

Down syndrome A child with Down syndrome has extra genetic material in each cell (an extra copy of chromosome 21). He or she often has a learning disability.

Epiglottis A flap of tissue at the entrance to the windpipe (trachea).

Esophagus The muscular tube leading from the mouth to the top of the stomach.

Fetal alcohol syndrome A child born to a mother who has drunk large amounts of alcohol in pregnancy can be blind and have an abnormally shaped face. This is known as fetal alcohol syndrome.

Gall bladder A sac-like organ that collects bile and releases it into the intestine after a fatty meal.

Ganglion A group of nerve cells.

Hormones Chemical messengers carried by blood from where they are made, to where they are needed.

Hypothalamus An area at the base of the brain which controls many of the body's automatic and hormone-related activities.

Immune system The complex system which the body uses to defend itself against infection.

Killer T cell A white blood cell, part of the immune system. It kills invaders by direct contact.

Lanugo The fine hair that covers a fetus from the fifth month of pregnancy until about the eighth month. It is lost before birth.

Ligaments The strong cords that link bones together at joints.

Liver An organ of the body, found at the top of the abdomen; aids in digestion and processing food.

Memory cells B cells or T cells that can divide to form a family of new cells, capable of fighting an infection, when they encounter antigens from a foreign organism.

Mitral valve The valve on the left side of the heart which allows blood to enter the left ventricle from the left atrium.

Morula A solid ball of about eight to fifty cells, produced in the first days after an egg is fertilized.

Motor nerves Nerves that carry information to the tissues from the brain.

Nicotine A chemical in tobacco. It binds to receptors in the brain when smoke is inhaled, producing a feeling of calm. It is addictive.

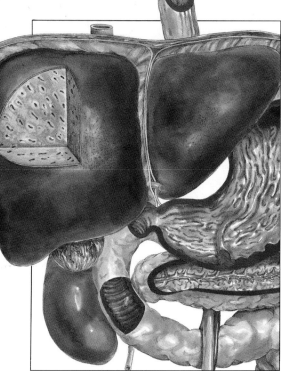

Ovaries Organs found in a woman's abdomen, which produce fertile eggs. An average woman produces 400 eggs in her lifetime.

Pancreas An organ in the abdomen that produces digestive enzymes and also the hormone, insulin.

Pituitary gland The gland in the brain that produces growth hormone.

Placenta The organ that attaches a growing fetus to its mother in her uterus. It carries food and oxygen from the mother to the fetus and takes away carbon dioxide.

Scarification Scraping the skin with the intention of leaving a scar. Used as a method of body decoration in Africa.

Sensory nerves Nerves that carry information to the brain from the tissues and organs.

Somatic nervous system The part of the nervous system which deals with body activities that are under our conscious control, for example, skeletal muscle movement.

Tendons The strong cords that link bones to muscles.

Thalamus Part of the brain found under the cerebrum and above the hypothalamus.

Tourniquet A tight bandage tied around an injured limb to stop it from bleeding.

Tricuspid valve The valve that allows blood to flow from the right atrium to the right ventricle.

Uterus The pear-shaped organ in a woman which holds the developing fetus during pregnancy.

Valve A mechanism that allows fluid to flow one way, but not the other, down a tube. The heart chambers and veins have valves.

Vein A blood vessel that carries blood from the tissues to the heart.

Vena cava The large vein by which blood returns to the heart from the tissues. It enters the heart in the right atrium.

Ventricles The two lower pumping chambers of the heart. The left ventricle pumps oxygenated blood to the body. The right ventricle pumps blood to the lungs.

Vitamin An essential nutrient that the body requires only in small quantities.

Zygote The cell formed by the fusion of an egg and a sperm.

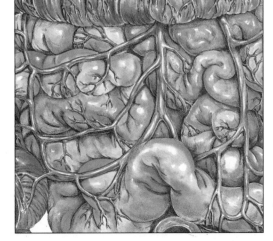

PRINTED IN BELGIUM BY
proost
INTERNATIONAL BOOK PRODUCTION

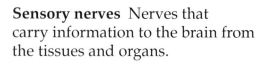

Hormones Chemical messengers carried by blood from where they are made, to where they are needed.

Hypothalamus An area at the base of the brain which controls many of the body's automatic and hormone-related activities.

Immune system The complex system which the body uses to defend itself against infection.

Killer T cell A white blood cell, part of the immune system. It kills invaders by direct contact.

Lanugo The fine hair that covers a fetus from the fifth month of pregnancy until about the eighth month. It is lost before birth.

Ligaments The strong cords that link bones together at joints.

Liver An organ of the body, found at the top of the abdomen; aids in digestion and processing food.

Memory cells B cells or T cells that can divide to form a family of new cells, capable of fighting an infection, when they encounter antigens from a foreign organism.

Mitral valve The valve on the left side of the heart which allows blood to enter the left ventricle from the left atrium.

Morula A solid ball of about eight to fifty cells, produced in the first days after an egg is fertilized.

Motor nerves Nerves that carry information to the tissues from the brain.

Nicotine A chemical in tobacco. It binds to receptors in the brain when smoke is inhaled, producing a feeling of calm. It is addictive.

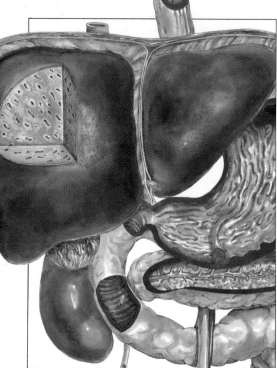

Ovaries Organs found in a woman's abdomen, which produce fertile eggs. An average woman produces 400 eggs in her lifetime.

Pancreas An organ in the abdomen that produces digestive enzymes and also the hormone, insulin.

Pituitary gland The gland in the brain that produces growth hormone.

Placenta The organ that attaches a growing fetus to its mother in her uterus. It carries food and oxygen from the mother to the fetus and takes away carbon dioxide.

Scarification Scraping the skin with the intention of leaving a scar. Used as a method of body decoration in Africa.

Sensory nerves Nerves that carry information to the brain from the tissues and organs.

Somatic nervous system The part of the nervous system which deals with body activities that are under our conscious control, for example, skeletal muscle movement.

Tendons The strong cords that link bones to muscles.

Thalamus Part of the brain found under the cerebrum and above the hypothalamus.

Tourniquet A tight bandage tied around an injured limb to stop it from bleeding.

Tricuspid valve The valve that allows blood to flow from the right atrium to the right ventricle.

Uterus The pear-shaped organ in a woman which holds the developing fetus during pregnancy.

Valve A mechanism that allows fluid to flow one way, but not the other, down a tube. The heart chambers and veins have valves.

Vein A blood vessel that carries blood from the tissues to the heart.

Vena cava The large vein by which blood returns to the heart from the tissues. It enters the heart in the right atrium.

Ventricles The two lower pumping chambers of the heart. The left ventricle pumps oxygenated blood to the body. The right ventricle pumps blood to the lungs.

Vitamin An essential nutrient that the body requires only in small quantities.

Zygote The cell formed by the fusion of an egg and a sperm.